KEN WHITE
MURALIST AND PAINTER

Angela Atkinson

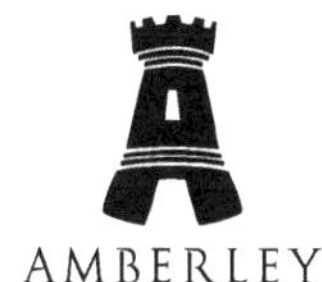

AMBERLEY

To my daughter Laura, without whom this book would not have been possible.

Ken White

First published 2019

Amberley Publishing
The Hill, Stroud
Gloucestershire, GL5 4EP

www.amberley-books.com

Copyright © Angela Atkinson, 2019

The right of Angela Atkinson to be identified as the Author
of this work has been asserted in accordance with the
Copyrights, Designs and Patents Act 1988.

All rights reserved. No part of this book may be reprinted
or reproduced or utilised in any form or by any electronic,
mechanical or other means, now known or hereafter invented, including photocopying and recording,
or in any information
storage or retrieval system, without the permission in writing
from the Publishers.

British Library Cataloguing in Publication Data.
A catalogue record for this book is available from the British Library.

ISBN 978 1 4456 9380 4 (print)
ISBN 978 1 4456 9381 1 (ebook)

Typesetting and Origination by Amberley Publishing.
Printed in Great Britain.

Appointed GPSR EU Representative: Easy Access System Europe Oü, 16879218
Address: Mustamäe tee 50, 10621, Tallinn, Estonia
Contact Details: gpsr.requests@easproject.com, +358 40 500 3575

Contents

Introduction

Swindon is a somewhat astonishing hot-bed of creativity of all kinds. It's one where wide-ranging performing arts rub shoulders with creative arts of every genre. Many of Swindon's creatives arrived in the town at various times in their lives; some moved on in later years, while others made the place their home and stayed. Others still are born Swindonians. Ken White, this book's subject, falls into the latter group.

The middle child of three, Ken entered the world in his grandparent's home, Gordon Gardens in Swindon on 23 March 1943.

Ken's father, George Albert White, served in the RAF as a Flight Sergeant physical training instructor before doing what so many of Swindon's men did and entered the GWR Works, as his father did before him and his sons after him. Yet Ken's determination to make his mark in the art world saw him eventually break away from the well-trodden path of Swindon's menfolk to a working life 'inside', as Swindonians referred to it.

The third generation of his family to enter the Works, the tender age of fifteen saw Ken begin his working life as a rivet hotter in the Carriage and Wagon Department. This was a dirty job, involving sustaining regular small burns from sparks dropping down his boots. Ken loathed it. Yet he was fortunate in not being too long in escaping that role, and beginning an artistic career of sorts as an apprentice signwriter in the same department. He started out freshening up existing signage before moving on to hone his skills writing new signage. The first apprentice for some time to get a transfer to signwriting, he found himself stencilling numbers on railway carriages before moving on to painting wagons and containers – one such being for Bird's Eye, requiring the text in actual gold leaf. When Ken paints today he still uses the palette he made back then, in the Works.

In later years, Ken produced a painting entitled *Signwriters*. Acquired by Swindon's STEAM museum, the work depicts his mentor and inspiration, 'Wee Georgie Bennet', working on the rolling stock. A vast improvement on working as a rivet hotter, Ken describes his time as a GWR signwriter as one of reasonable contentment. But it wasn't quite enough, so alongside that role, and by now aged seventeen, he went to evening classes at Swindon Art College to study O and A-Level art, with the avowed intention of becoming a full-time artist.

Fast forward to 1962 and the nineteen-year-old Ken left the Works to enrol in a full-time, four-year-long art diploma course at Swindon Art College. It's not hard to understand how this move would have been against the wishes of his parents. For the working classes in this era, the ultimate goal in life, and the dearest wish for their children, was a 'steady job' and the security that accompanied it. Entering the art world represented none of that. Many of that generation were familiar with the (not without truth) cliché of the artist starving in a garret in the manner of Vincent Van Gogh. And who would want that for their children? The attitude of parents like Ken's, though with the best of intentions of course, created conflict with offspring keen to follow their own desires.

Yet Ken, committed and focused, only ever wanted to draw and paint. Besides which, by his own admission, it's the only thing he was ever any good at.

At length, Ken's ambitions of working as a full-time artist reached fruition with work as a muralist and leading exponent of the art of *Trompe-l'œil*. Over the course of his mural painting career Ken created over 100 murals across the world, with at least ten being in his home town. The pity is that only one now remains there – the Golden Lion Mural. However, it is fitting that this should be the one to remain, given its pivotal role in events for Ken.

But how did Ken make the transition from 1960s art student to muralist and acclaimed *Trompe-l'œil* artist – aside from his undisputable talent and undoubted hard work that is, because talent, as we know, is not enough on its own. Which rather returns to the whole starving-artist-suffering-for-his-art thing, and that begs the question: what made the difference for him? Why was Ken successful when so many painters, singers, actors – you name it – are not? A confluence of factors is what. If ever there was a case of 'in-the-right-place-at-the-right-time-with-the-right-people', Ken's is it.

Ken's personal perfect storm includes the town of his birth and the creative opportunities it afforded during the 1970s and 1980s, a pivotal boyhood friendship, the political climate of the time, having several art college friends who just so happened to go on to fame and fortune in the pop world and a certain advertisement run by international pharmaceutical and paint company Bayer.

Then of course there's the singular factor of Ken's twenty-year working relationship with a well-known entrepreneur by the name of Richard Branson – what one might call a big break in and of itself. And yet, while far from incidental to Ken's career, there's an argument that all of the above had to have happened first. Indeed, when examining Ken's trajectory, the nursery rhyme 'For want of a nail the shoe was lost' springs to mind. By the end of the rhyme a kingdom is lost for the want of a horse shoe nail. Happily for Ken though, he lost nothing and gained everything, but you get the idea; one thing builds on another. The Branson/White relationship is far from being Ken's whole picture, and all this, this book will examine.

Some of the 100 murals Ken painted worldwide were for well-heeled and well-known patrons – one such being a 1984 commission from investment banker Jacob Rothschild. He set our man to painting a 60-foot-tall faux Georgian townhouse façade on the Royal Opera House, overlooking the Jubilee Gardens Piazza in Covent Garden. Indeed, throughout the 1980s Ken the muralist became a familiar London sight, working on Park Lane's Intercontinental Hotel, Madame Tussauds, Heathrow Airport and Kensington and Chelsea Pools.

Throughout this period Ken also travelled the world, brightening Branson's airport lounges, record shops and more with his murals. However, there is much more to Ken's work than murals; posters for Swindon events, lino cuts, music album covers and more all feature in his output. Now, in the 2000s, Ken's work focuses on paintings of life in and around the Works – the Swindon of the 1940s and 1950s.

Chapter 1

The 1960s: Ken Goes to Art College

Swindon, then, has a long history of creativity. Indeed, the amount of talent sent forth into the creative world by the town borders on astonishing. Among its glitterati one can count, in no particular order, official war artist Leslie Cole, musicians Gilbert O'Sullivan and Rick Davies of Supertramp fame. Another, born in neighbouring Wroughton (1901–66), is Hubert Cook, who worked as a machinist in Swindon's Works until 1944. He became best known for his lithographs, purchased by New York's Metropolitan Museum and the War Artist's Advisory Committee – not a talentless rollcall by any stretch, and one that makes only the dimmest of daubs on Swindon's canvas.

Going some way to explain the town's prolific artistic output is Swindon College's backstory. Back in 1896 a Day Secondary School for boys opened in the newly built Victoria Road Technical School. In 1899 the school had a workshop and engineering laboratory added. Until 1952 this building housed both a technical college and secondary school when school-age pupils transferred to the new Headlands School. Swindon's art school came into being in this Victorian building in the early 1900s – maybe earlier. For over thirty years it had Harold Dearden at its helm. Dearden studied at the Rochdale School of Art from 1905 to 1910, then at London's Royal College of Art. By the time Ken went to the art school to start his night classes in the 1960s, it had moved to a new Swindon College building around the corner on Regent Circus.

In 1960 Ken undertook first his O and A-Levels in art, followed by a four-year art diploma course in a long-established college with a reputation for nurturing and producing talented artists. Ken's course covered all the main creative/artistic disciplines with lessons including printing and wood engraving – those from his mentor Ken Lindley – and Japanese-style woodcuts.

The first two years of Ken's studies then comprised timetabled, set classes. For the second half of the diploma the students could choose to work in whatever medium they chose. It's no surprise to hear that Ken opted to study working with oils. Had you been around at the time, you'd have found the willing-to-learn Ken in the college building well into the night, with the caretaker being the only other person there.

Reminiscing about those days, Ken comments how wonderful going to college was when compared to life in the Works. He recalls too, how when first he started at college staff pushed him into doing graphics work – but sneaked, unbeknownst to college staff, to the top floor art room to paint.

Location, Location, Location

This book's introduction spoke of Ken's stroke of Richard Branson-shaped fortune – an element of Ken's perfect storm to examine again later. But the first contributing factor to Ken's success lay in his birthplace – the town that is, not his home and early school life. As he himself says, both of those things were less than satisfactory. Infant school Ken describes as rough, with teachers that were the antithesis of encouraging. There he enjoyed only two subjects: history and art. Ken loathed sport and most other subjects to boot, and lived for the art lessons. Junior School saw him appear in the local paper with one of his paintings. That marked a high point; an epiphany even. Along with the praise for this piece of work came the realisation that here was something he was good at. And with that was ignited a fierce longing to paint professionally.

By dint of being born and brought up in a town that happened to have this excellent art college, Ken's talent and determination received the best of help. No matter the extent of his talent and the strength of his ambition and his willingness to work hard, Ken would surely have faced a harder battle to achieve it had he not happened to have a long-established and excellent art school right on his doorstep.

Getting By with a Little Help from His Friends

As is so often the case with our college years, Ken formed enduring friendships during his. What differs with Ken, however, is that the friends he made went on to become household names. Not everyone can claim one pop personality as a friend, let alone two. One such was the future Supertramp keyboardist Rick Davies, and yet another was Gilbert (Ray) O'Sullivan. They'd often escape the art room and decamp to Rick's town centre flat to play vinyl records at full blast. Ken, Rick and Ray all did the same course in Swindon Art College. They too play their part in Ken's output, and by extension his success.

But the most important relationship to come out of art college had to be Jan, his girlfriend and later his wife. Ken admits to admiring Jan from afar for quite some time but being too shy to talk to her. Until one party in nearby Marlborough that was ... and the rest, as the saying goes, is history.

After Graduation

On leaving college, Ken did what any aspiring artist in the 1960s would do and went to London to work for the British Council as an exhibition designer – exactly the kind of steady job his family yearned for him to have. He also worked as a freelance commercial artist and illustrator and hawked his folder of work around the offices of magazines and book publishing houses in the city, in the hope of getting commissions. During this time he worked on a short-lived mural on the Apple clothing shop in London.

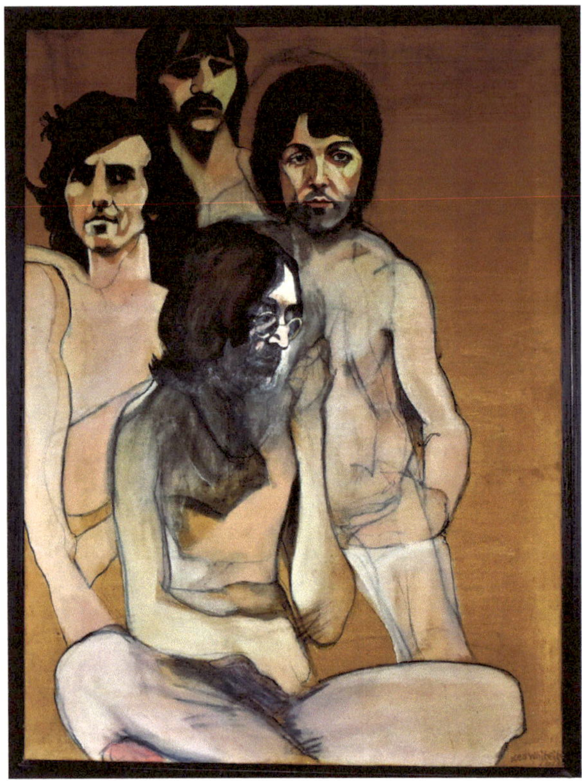

The Beatles from the book cover of the *Beatles Illustrated Lyrics* by Alan Aldridge.

The Beatles figured in Ken's career again in 1969. In that year, an artist, illustrator and graphic designer by the name of Alan Aldridge put together *The Beatles Illustrated Lyrics*, published in 1970. Aldridge advertised in the *Evening Standard* for drawings of the group. Ken responded with a painting of the Beatles naked. Aldridge paid him £20 for the reproduction rights in the book and even offered him £100 for the original. The canny Ken declined to sell and still has the painting today.

A year later, in 1970, Ken and Jan married and moved to Watford for her to undertake a teacher training course. For his part, Ken commuted daily to the city before finding work in Bristol.

As the years passed and as family commitments allowed, Jan pursued her teaching career, in arts and crafts in the first instance. It was Jan who knitted many of the jazzy sweaters so synonymous with Branson during the 1970s and '80s.

Later, with two young children in tow, the couple had a period in New Zealand. Here, Ken did on-the-spot drawings for the *Auckland Herald* newspaper and illustrations for women's magazines. Though aware of the Pop Art and American Abstraction movements of the time, Ken's interests at this time lay in Akhnaten and Egyptian art.

The images that follow represent a small selection of his work from the 1960s. There are drawings of pop artists and celebrities of the day along with illustrations for iconic magazines of the time such as the feminist magazine *Spare Rib*, which ran from 1972 to 1993, *Intro Magazine*, first published in 1967, and *New Society Magazine*.

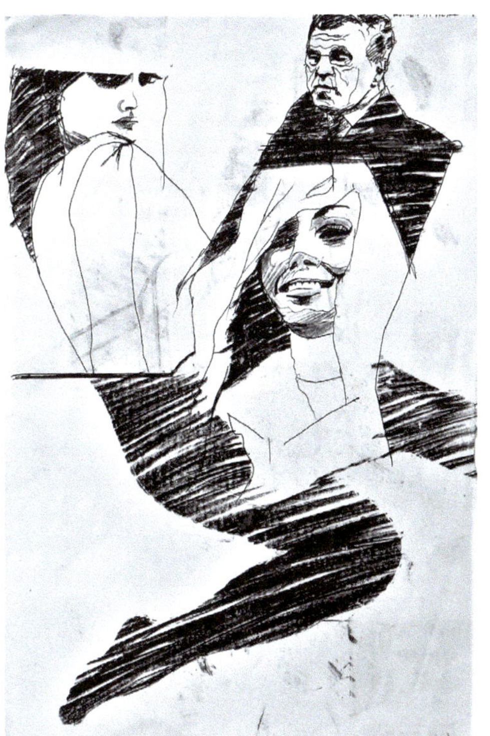

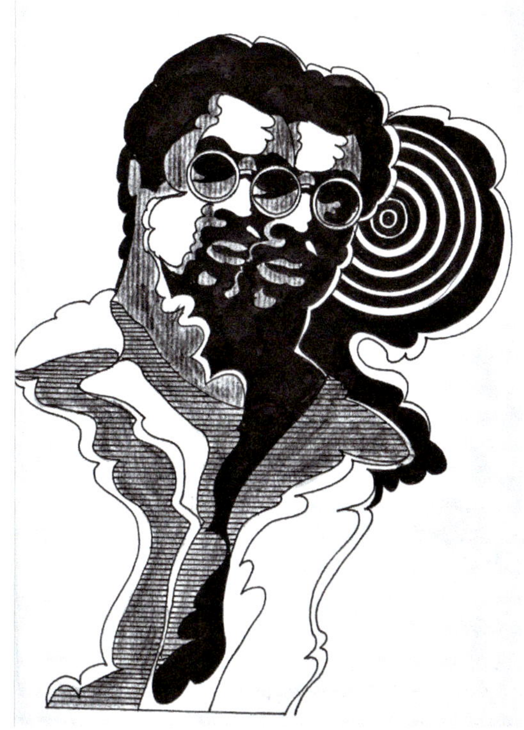

Above left and right: During his time at art school Ken produced various sketches to build his portfolio.

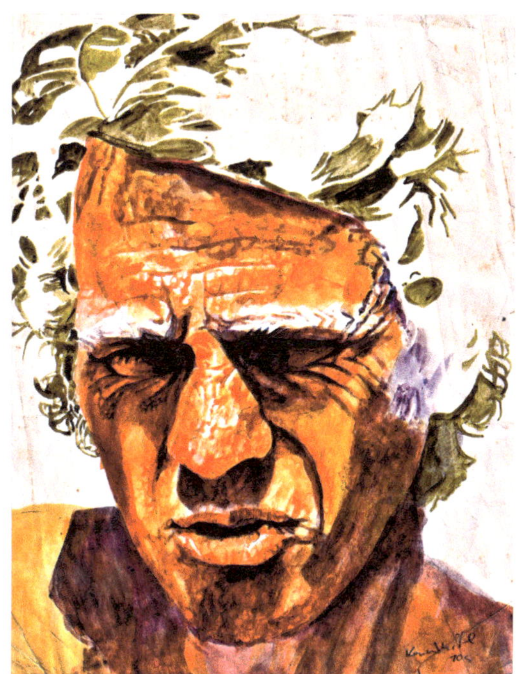

Steve McQueen from an art school drawing.

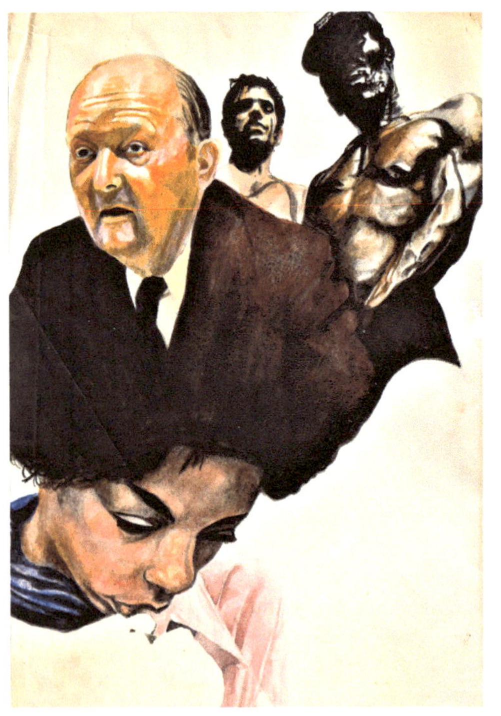

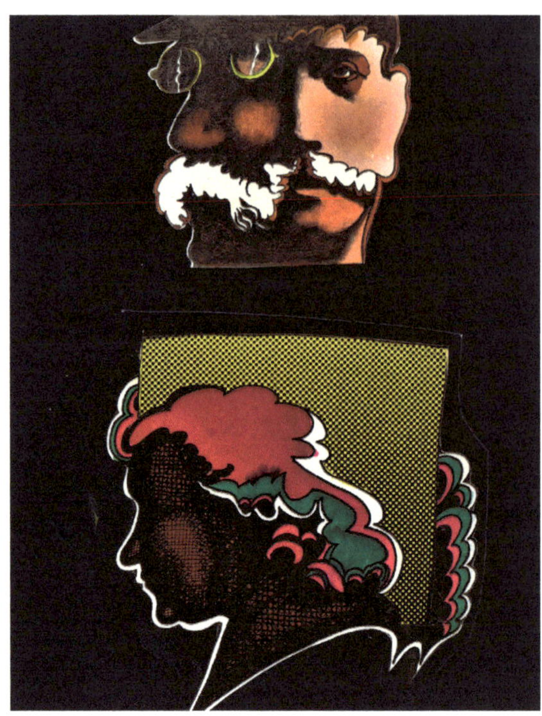

Above left, right and below: Sketch pad doodles.

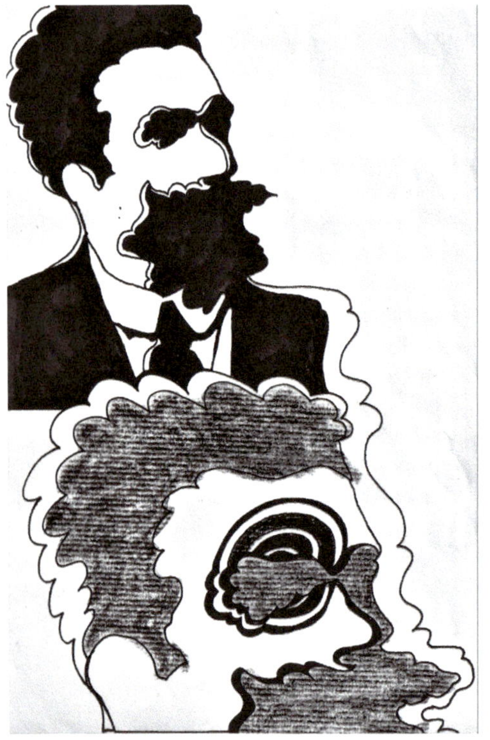

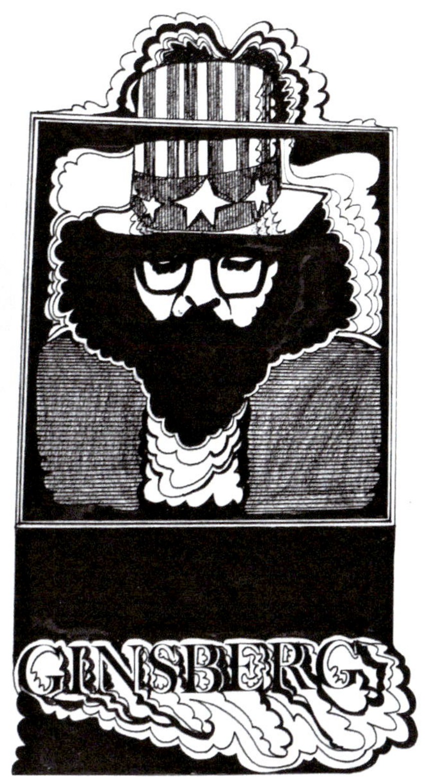

Allen Ginsberg from Ken's art school sketch pad
doodles created to build his portfolio.

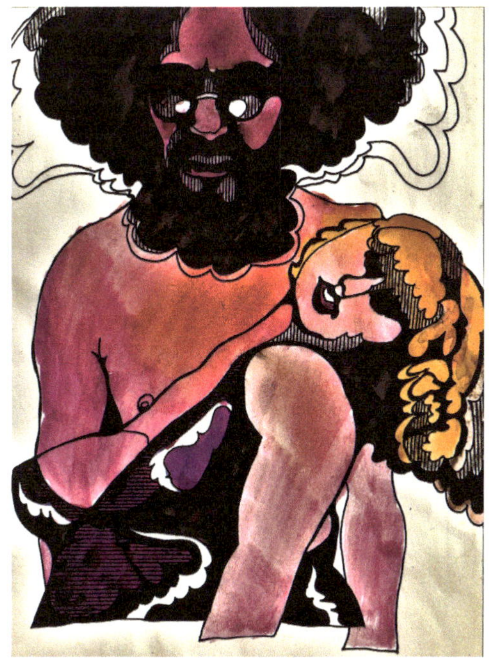

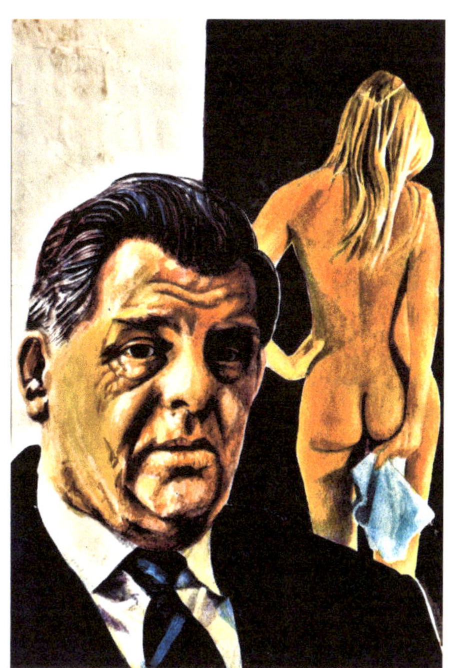

Above left and right: Sketch pad doodles.

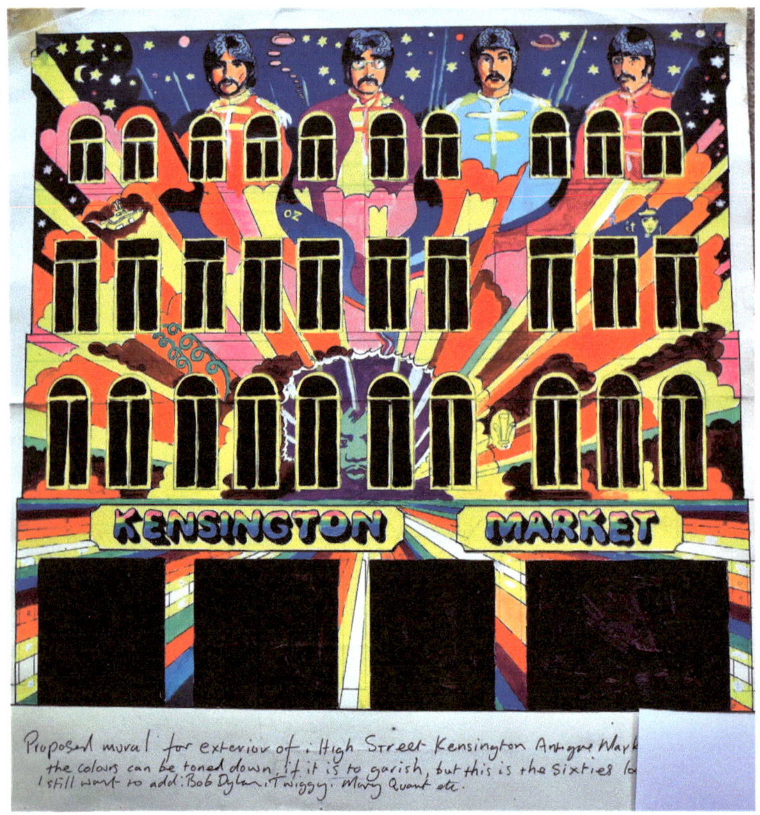

Proposal for
a mural in
Kensington market.

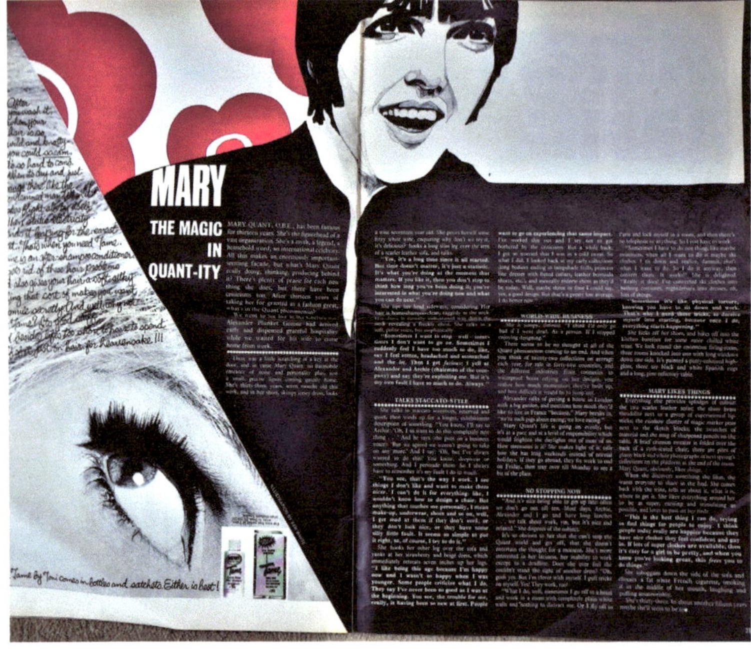

Mary Quant
illustration in
Intro magazine,
7 October 1967.

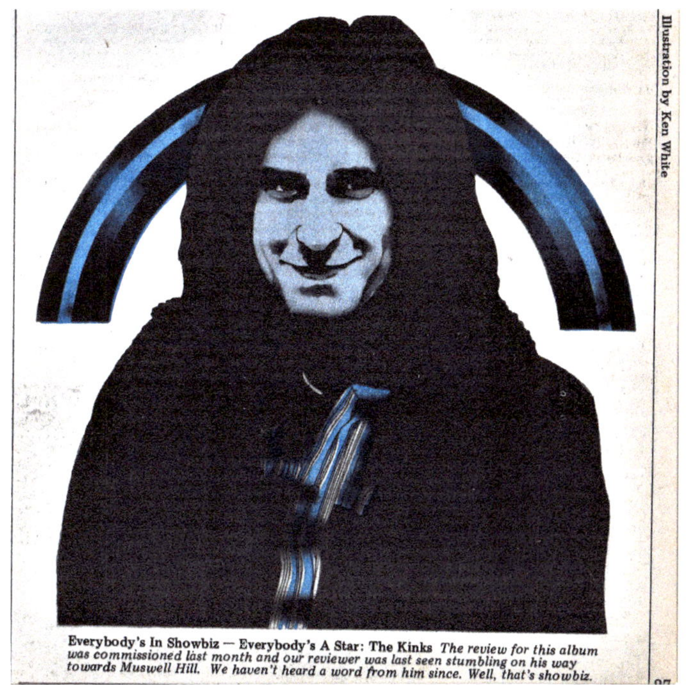

Everybody's In Showbiz — Everybody's A Star: The Kinks *The review for this album was commissioned last month and our reviewer was last seen stumbling on his way towards Muswell Hill. We haven't heard a word from him since. Well, that's showbiz.*

Ray Davis illustration in *Oz* magazine, November 1972.

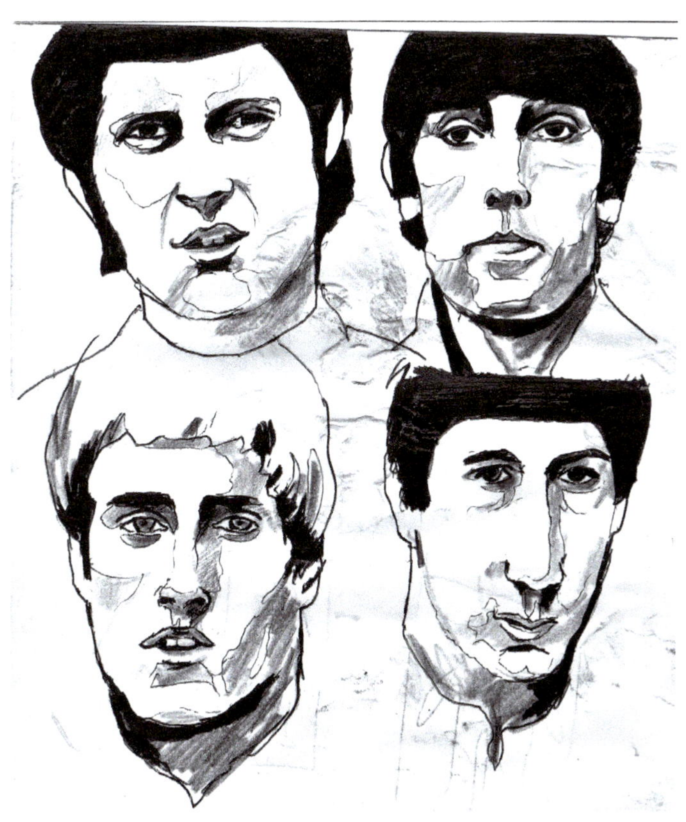

An art school drawing of The Who.

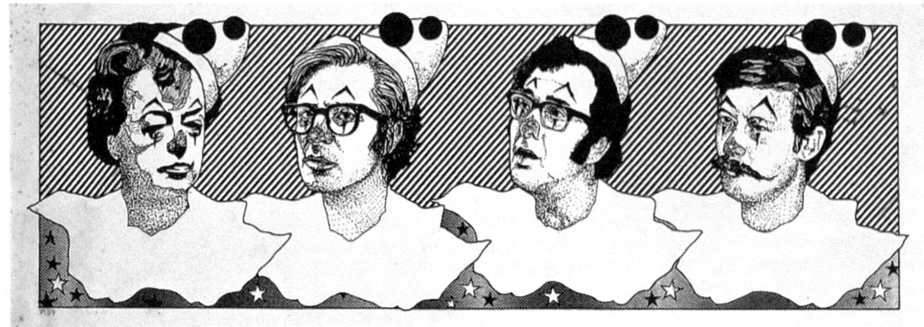

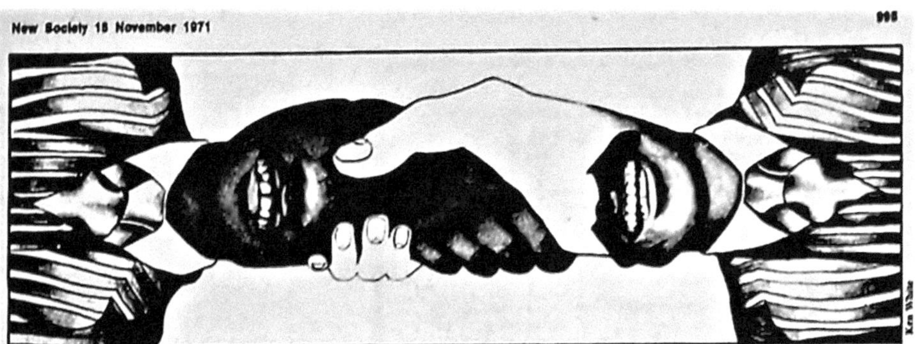

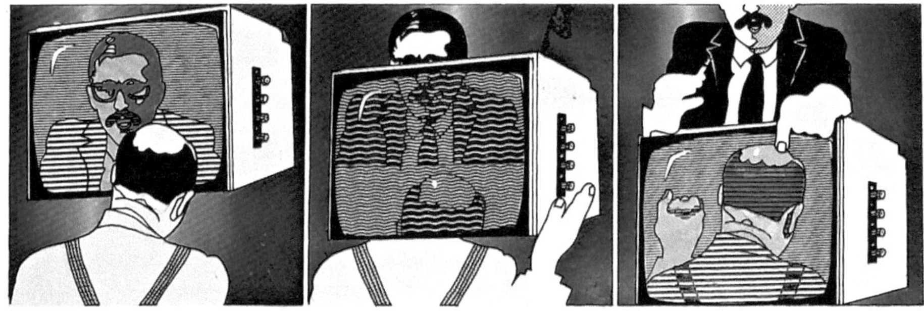

Illustration in *New Society* magazine in 1971.

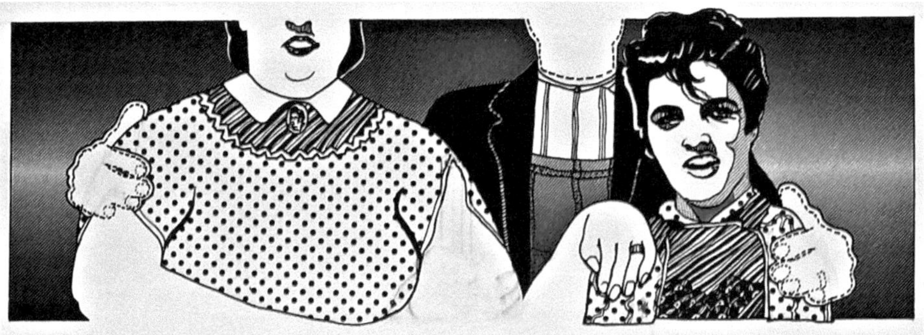

Ken drew this for an article on the Oedipus complex.

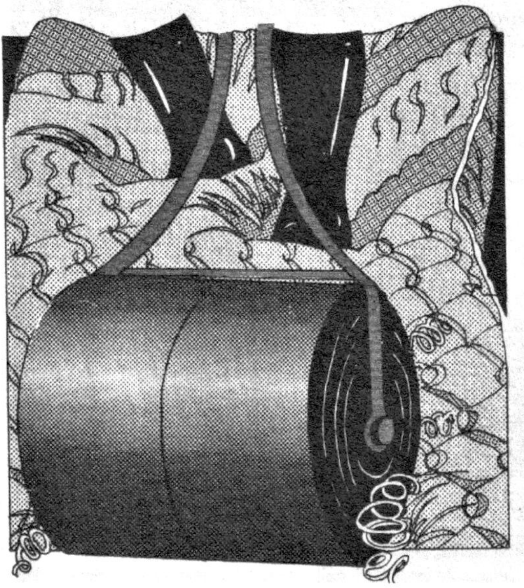

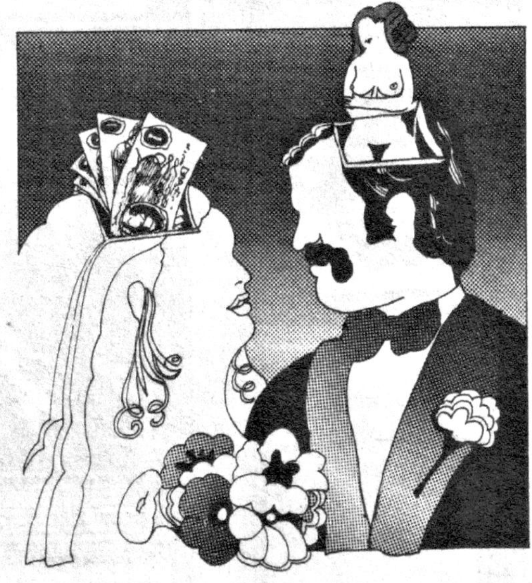

Above: *Spare Rib* was a landmark feminist magazine from the UK that ran from 1972 to 1993. This illustration accompanied the news section of the magazine.

Right: Illustration to accompany the news section of *Spare Rib* magazine in October 1972.

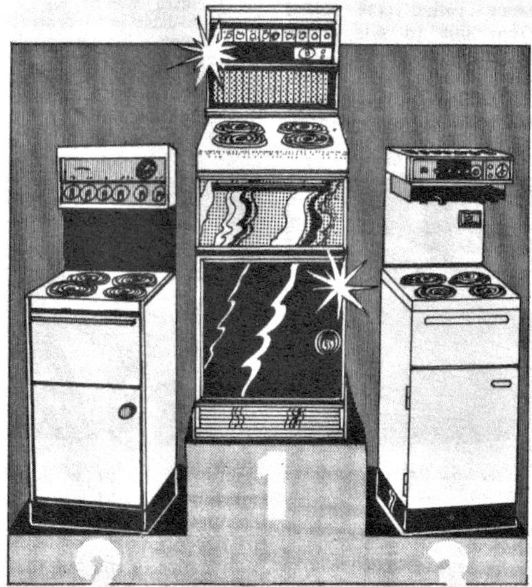

Ours is a consumer society. A consumer is one of the buying public. You are a consumer, and the chances are that you are an ignorant one. Ignorant of your rights, of the laws that exist for your protection and of the alternatives available in the goods and services you buy.

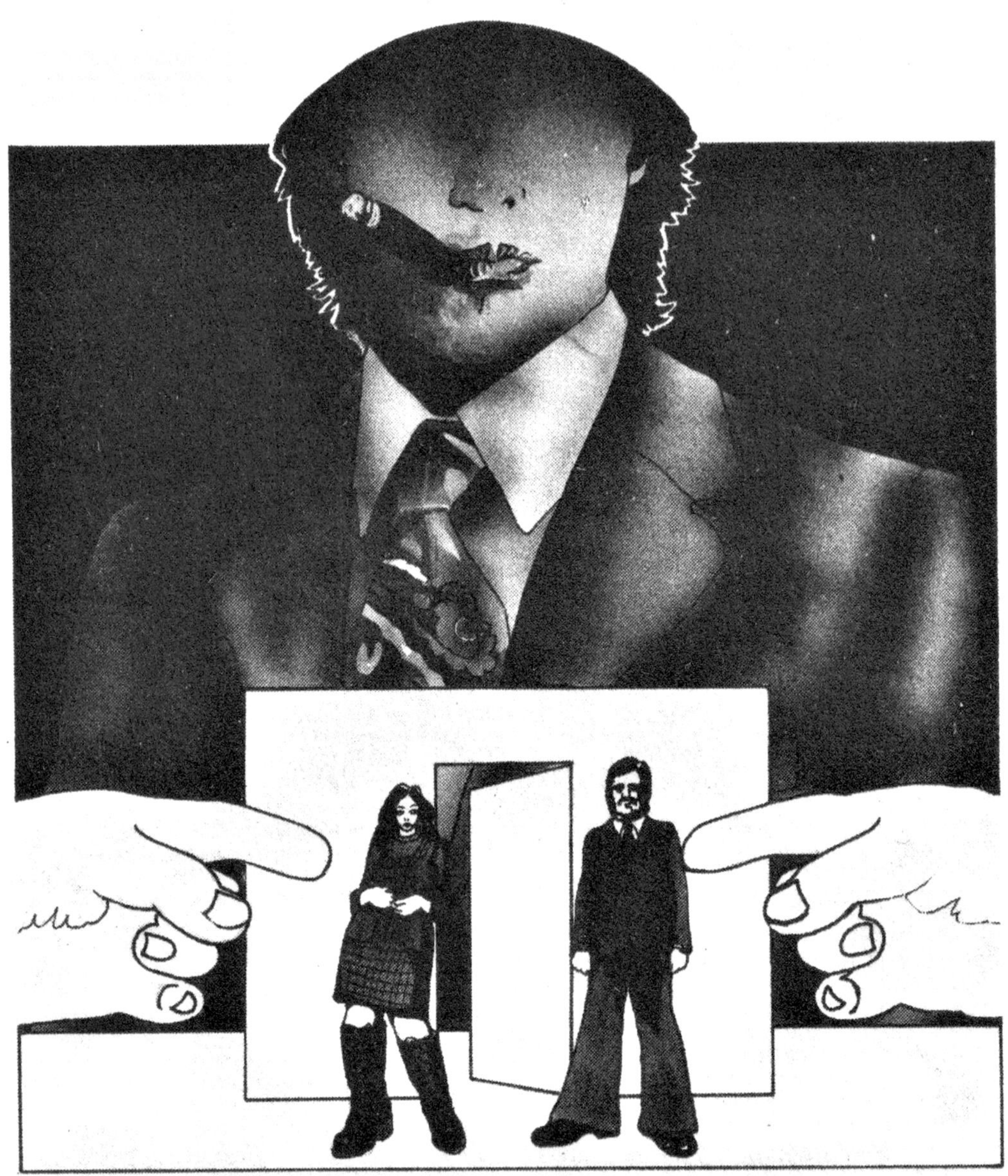

Ken White

Proposals have been put forward for the formation of a discrimination board in England. Here Michael Fogarty examines these proposals and assesses how effective such a board could be.

Illustration to accompany the news section of *Spare Rib* magazine in December 1972

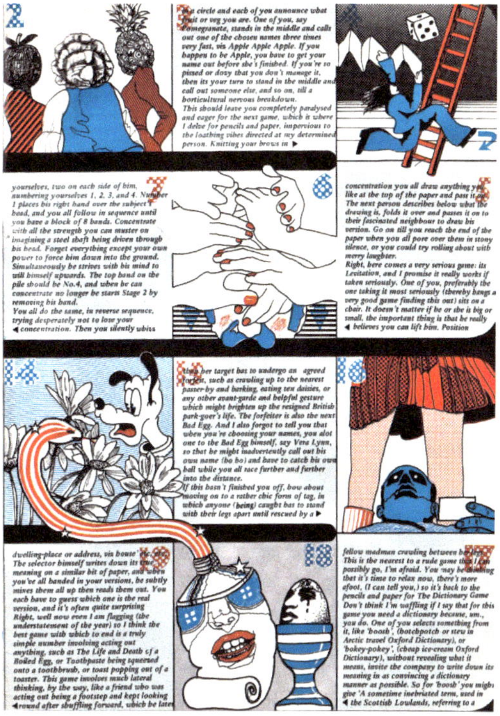

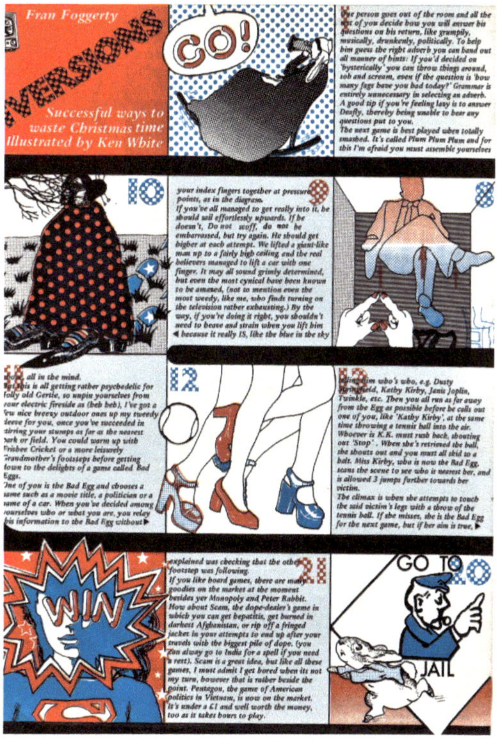

A double page spread illustration to accompany the article 'Successful Ways to Waste Christmastime' in *Spare Rib* magazine, January 1973.

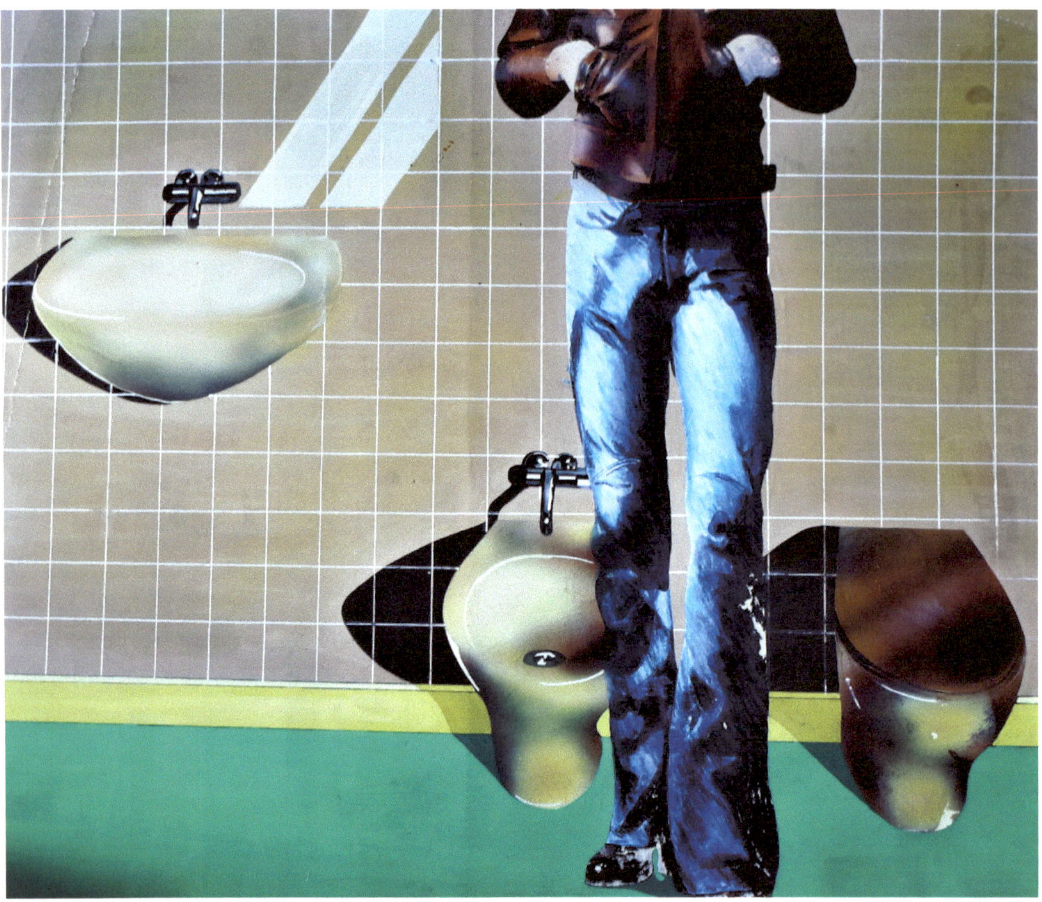

Jeans painting mid-1970s.

Chapter 2

Swindon Does Art

The Swindon Murals: Surrealism Comes to Swindon

Ken achieved worldwide acclaim for his mural work, with his *Trompe-l'œil* skills earning him an international reputation. The Great Western Railway aside, one can argue that Ken White as a muralist became one of Swindon's most successful exports. Yet, while these far-off places lauded his accomplishments, Swindon, until later in his career at least, remained a mite indifferent towards them.

Out of the ten or so murals Ken painted in Swindon, only one remains. This is his first – and a pivotal one at that. When the paint and pharmaceutical company Bayer ran an advertising campaign centred on colour, they used Ken's mural, with himself in the foreground. The advert ran on all the double-page adverts the company had in the Sunday supplements at the time and it got Ken noticed.

The Golden Lion Mural

In this mural Ken recreated, on an end terrace wall at the junction of Princes Street and Fleming Way, a street scene centred on the Golden Lion Bridge. Until its demolition in 1918, the bridge stood in Regent Street and spanned the Wilts & Berks Canal.

Ken took the scene from an old photograph dated around 1908. The photograph depicts a canal-side backdrop that includes the Regent Street branch of the Wilts & Dorset Bank, while in a terrace across the waterway there's the cottage home of the local chimney sweep, William Crick. Posed on and beside the bridge, wearing their Sunday-best clothes, are around thirty children.

In Ken's emulsion paint version, he replaced some of the children with some of Swindon's long-gone worthies. He included a glimpse of the Golden Lion public house and built Isambard Kingdom Brunel's famous stove-pipe hat into one of the stanchions. He also included poet Alfred Williams (AKA the Hammer Man poet – see *Secret Swindon* by the author) to commemorate the 1877 centenary of his birth.

This last remaining mural of Ken's underwent restoration in the 1980s and a full renovation by Ken in 2009 at the request of Swindon Borough Council and with funding from the Swindon Does Art project.* At this point he made some changes to the picture, added a light source and shadows, and used brighter colours throughout the mural.

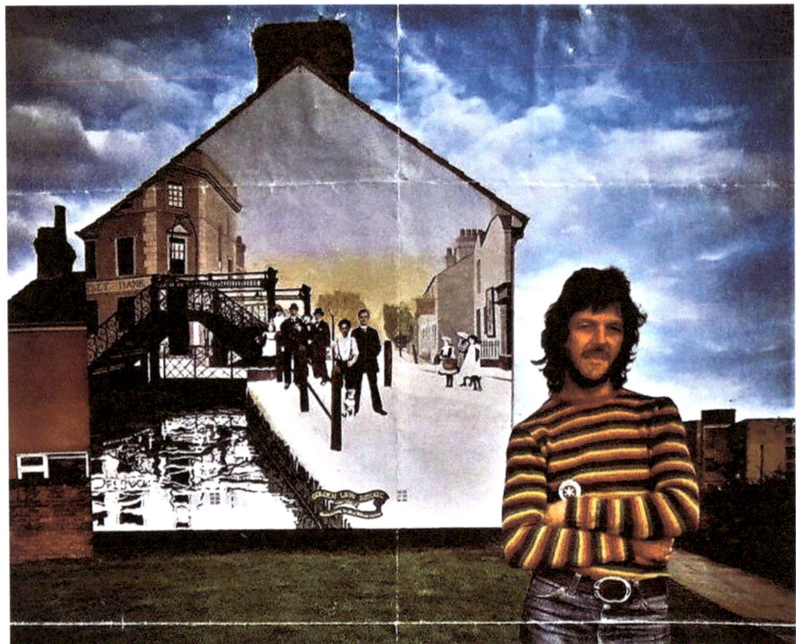

Ken standing in front of the Golden Lion mural in 1976.

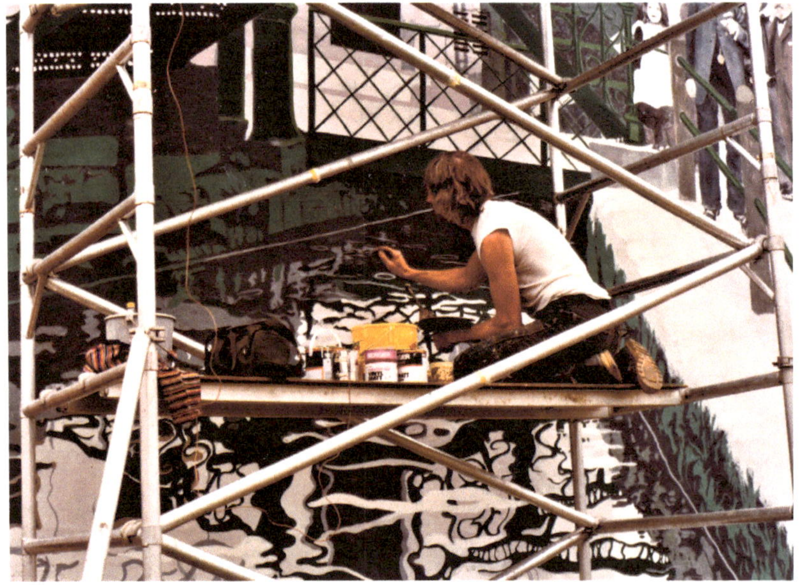

Ken working on the mural's bridge.

*Established in 2008, Swindon Does Art was a Swindon Borough Council initiative to help community art and creative activities while increasing public awareness of Swindon's broad spectrum of arts.

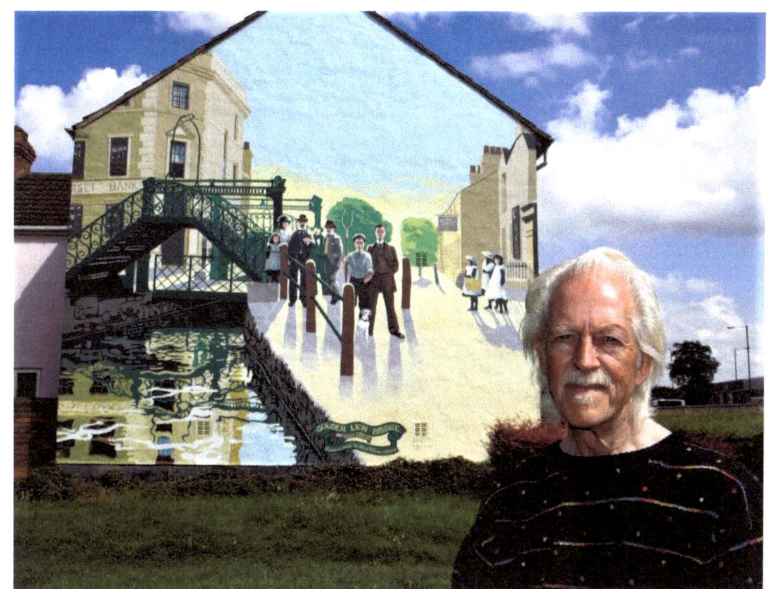

Ken White standing in front of the Golden Lion bridge mural after he'd reworked it. (Roger Ogle, *Swindon Link* magazine, 2006)

Rebuilding the Golden Lion Bridge

Terry Court, the boyhood friend referred to earlier, played a critical role in Ken White's career as Ken painted his first mural on a job creation programme run by Thamesdown Community Arts under Terry Court's direction in his arts officer capacity. His role had the rather grand and socialist sounding official title of 'Head of Thamesdown Cultural Policies' – a position he held for nigh on twenty years. Yet Terry was the antithesis of the highbrow arts director with his 'arts for everyone' ethos.

Now Ken's story touches the national political climate, whereby the 1970s Labour Government put in place job creation schemes as part of their attack on the problem of long-term unemployment.

Against this political backdrop, Terry had the idea of brightening up drab areas of Swindon with emulsion backdrops in the form of a series of colourful murals. Thus, he opened the door for Ken to rebuild the long-demolished Golden Lion Bridge in mural form. The Borough of Thamesdown, using the Labour Government's job creation scheme, financed Ken's involvement in the project to the tune of £25 a week – for which he had also to teach young students as the project progressed.

Throughout all this work in Swindon, Terry hadn't gone unnoticed in other places. Preferring to stay in Swindon, however, he turned down the chance to work for the Greater London Council. Indeed, its former leader, Ken Livingstone, once observed amazement at Swindon's achievements in public participation in art compared to those of the GLC. London's loss was Swindon's gain. Having eschewed the capital, Swindon benefitted from his inspired approach – an approach that saw he and Marie McClusky install both dance studios and artist studios in Swindon's Town Hall on Regent Circus. Ken had one of these studios for a time, *c.* 1974, alongside Carleton Attwood – another well-known, home-grown artist and sculptor.

Terry then introduced, and Ken painted, a programme that saw a series of eye-catching murals appear around town – transforming Swindon for a decade or so into the unlikely Murals Capital of the UK. Showing poor artistry of their own, the town's management failed to capitalise on this paintbrush-given opportunity to make Swindon a destination.

Ken recalls that, had it not been for Terry doing what he did at that stage, he might well have ended up as a gardener or working in some other random occupation. He describes Terry as an inspirational figure for Swindon's arts and culture. 'He was so good at sourcing grants for everything that went on here during the 1970s and '80s. He had dedication and made so much happen in Swindon.'

Swindon Events

But the work that Ken and Terry did together wasn't limited to murals. Terry used his position to instigate what many see as Swindon's golden era of arts – one that included street theatre, poetry reading, rock and jazz concerts, alternative and open-air cinema, and a huge assortment of cultural events and festivals. And it was to Ken Terry turned to produce a variety of promotional posters for these events – images of some them follow along with some images of non-Swindon related posters.

Ken's story doesn't merely touch on Swindon's creative activity during that period – it's welded to it as firmly as the rivets on a GWR locomotive.

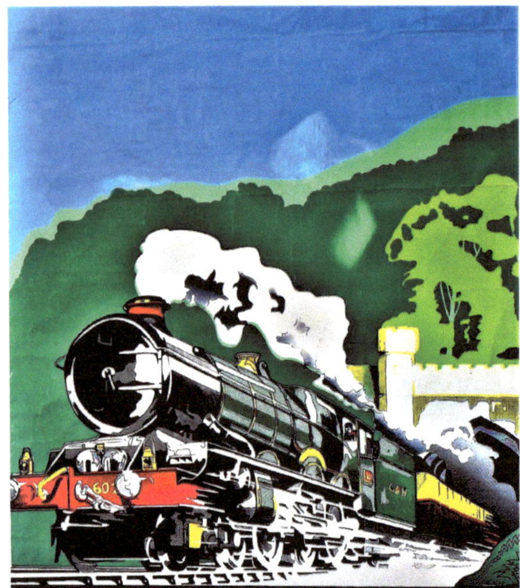

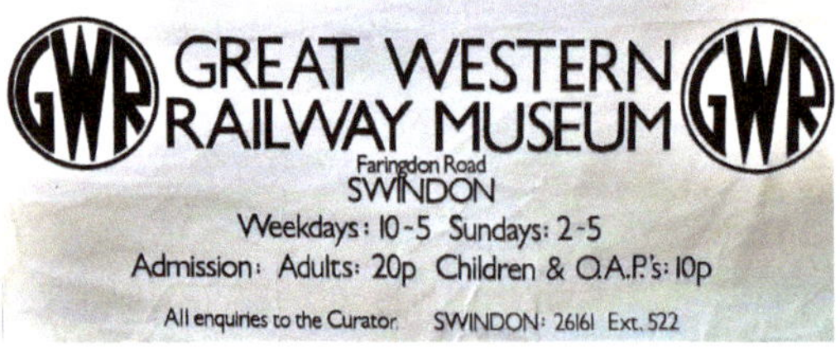

A poster for the GWR Museum in Faringdon Road. The museum is now STEAM and is by the McArthur Glen outlet centre.

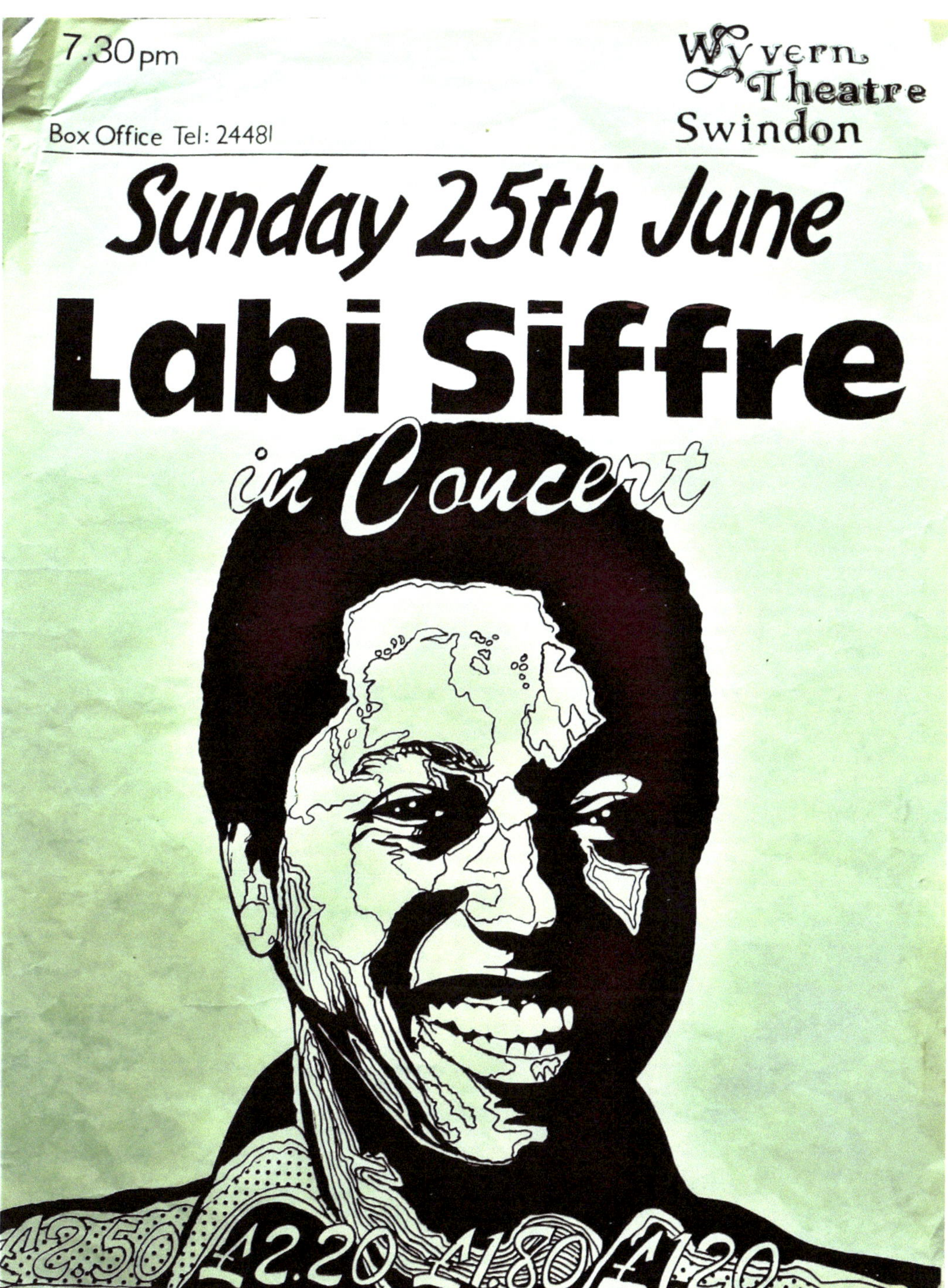

Labi Siffre at the Wyvern Theatre.

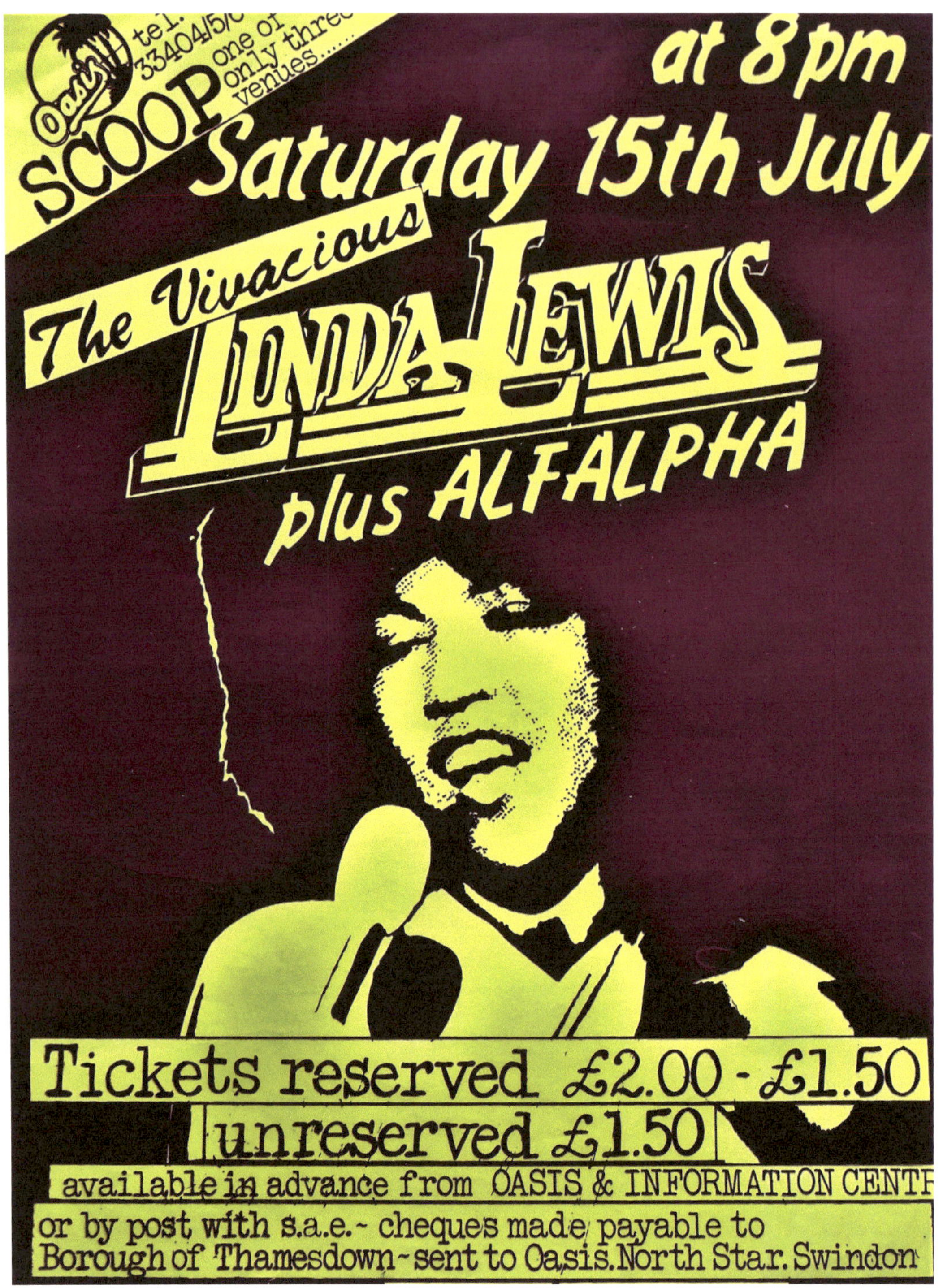

Linda Lewis at The Oasis.

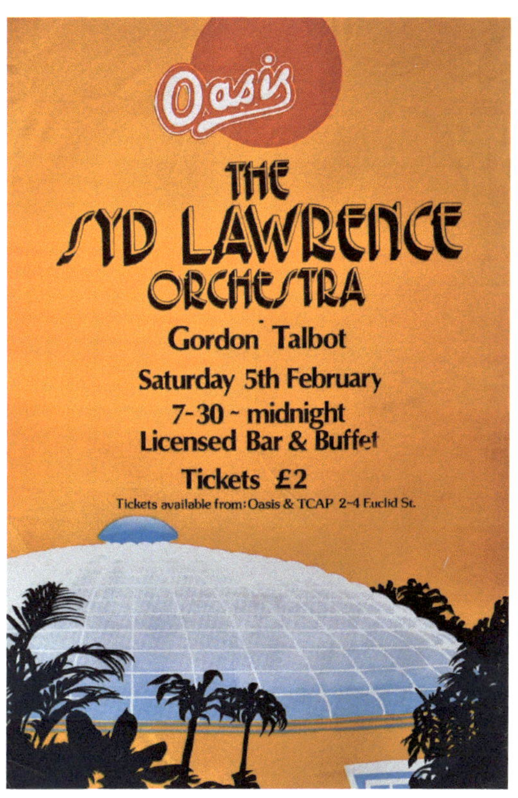

The Syd Lawrence Orchestra at The Oasis.

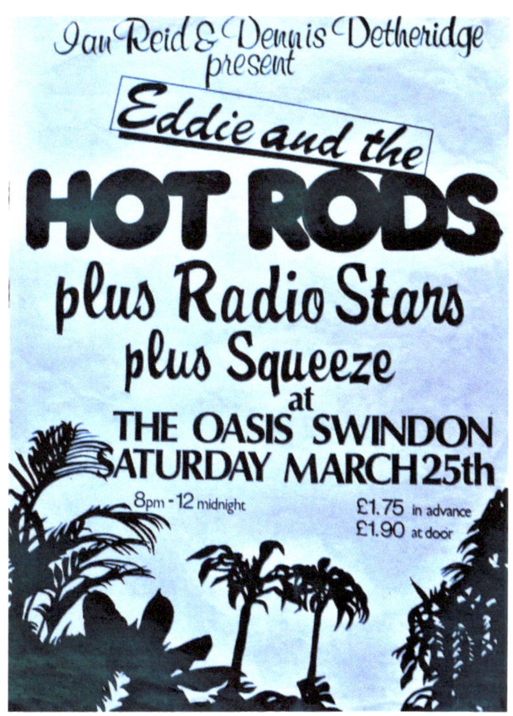

Eddie and the Hot Rods at The Oasis.

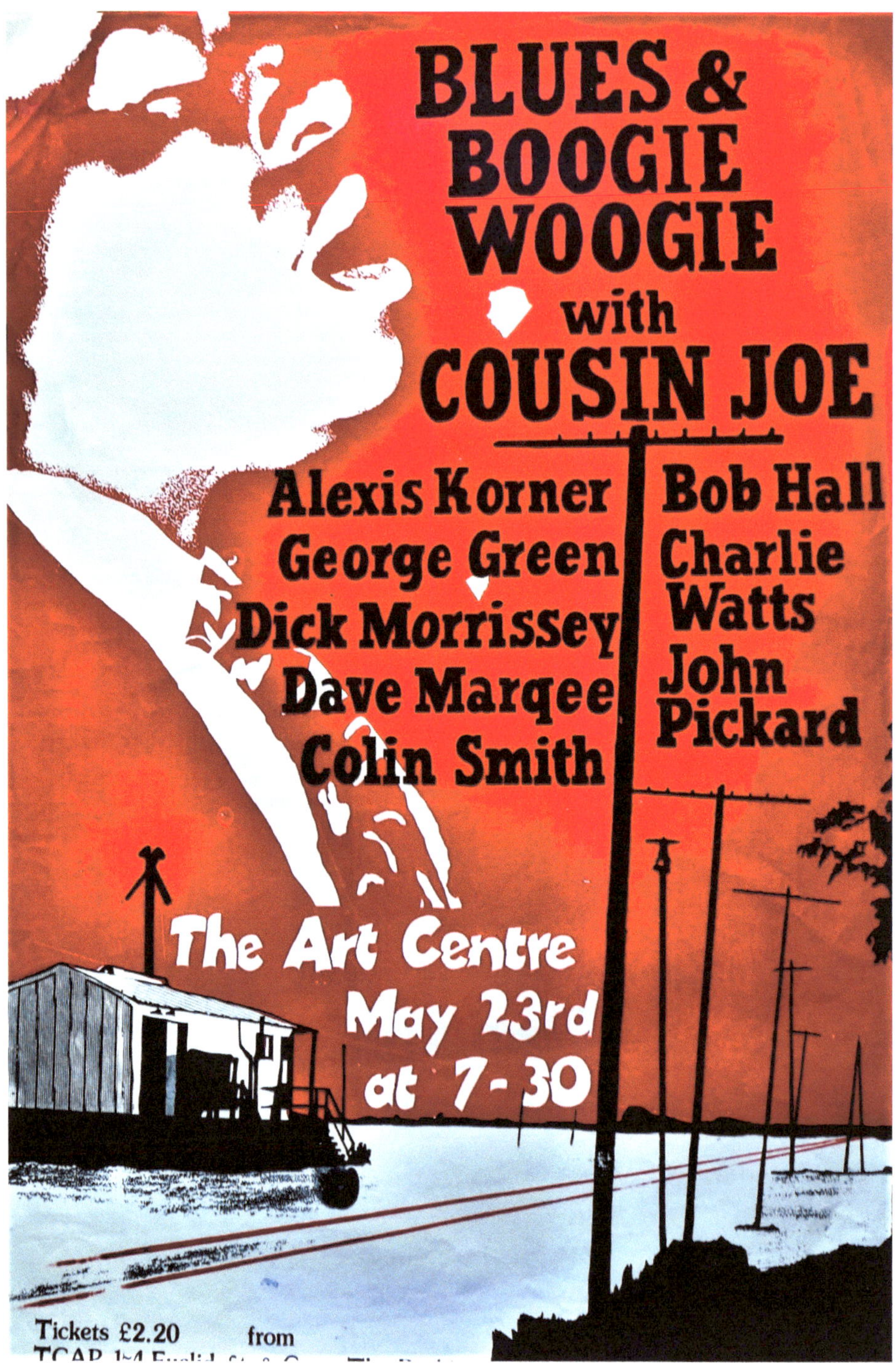

Blues and Boogie Woogie at the Arts Centre.

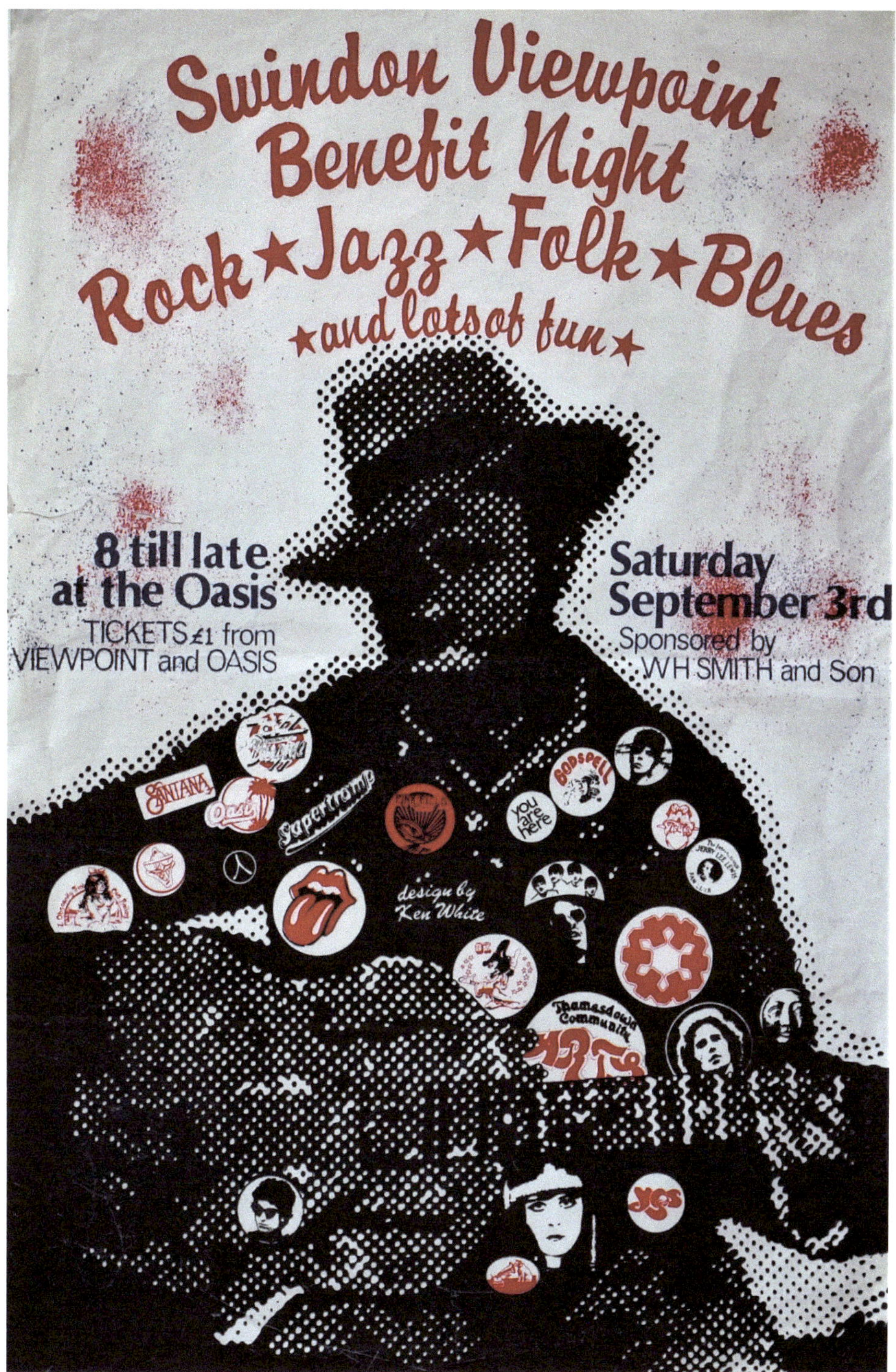

Swindon Viewpoint Benefit Night at The Oasis.

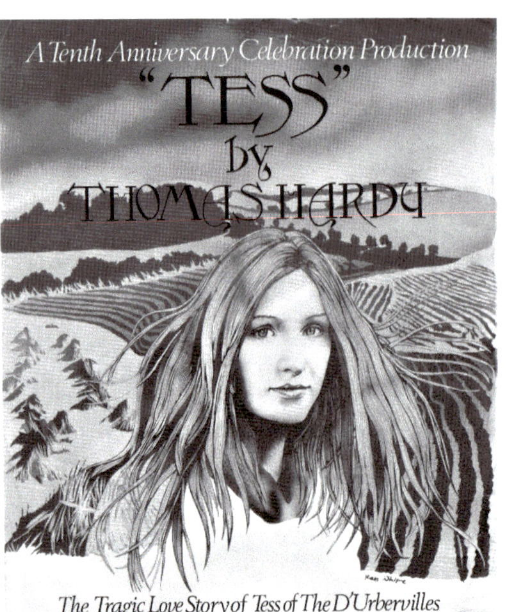

Tess by Thomas Hardy at the Wyvern
Theatre, 1981.

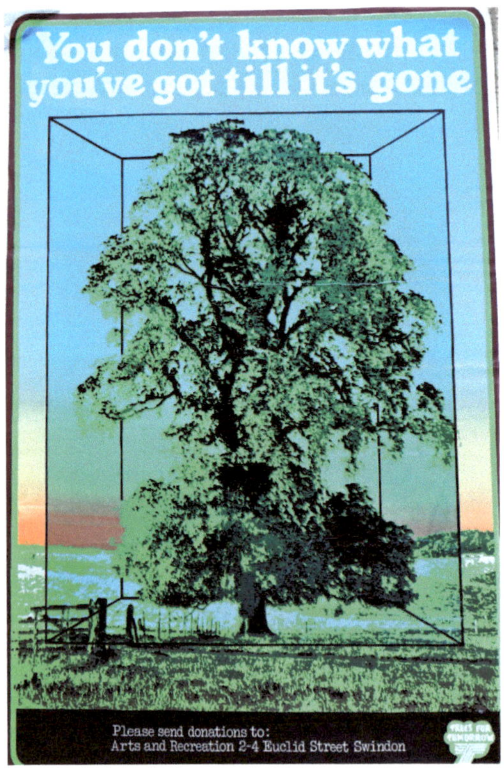

Swindon Arts and Recreation poster.

A Selection of Ken's non Swindon-related Posters

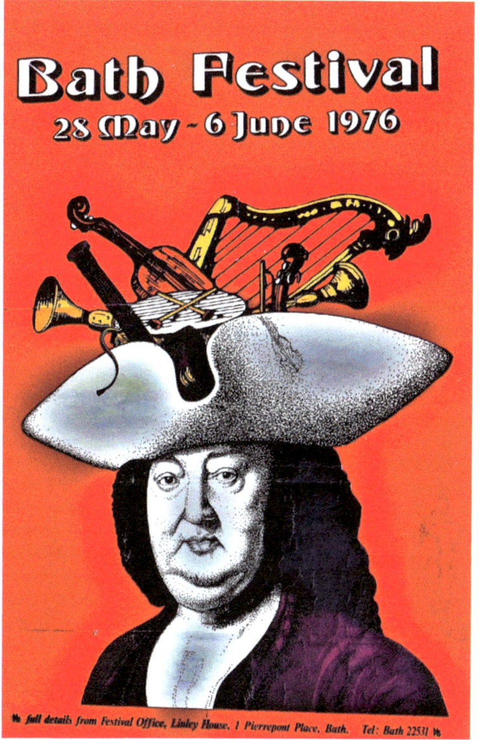

The Bath Festival, 1976.

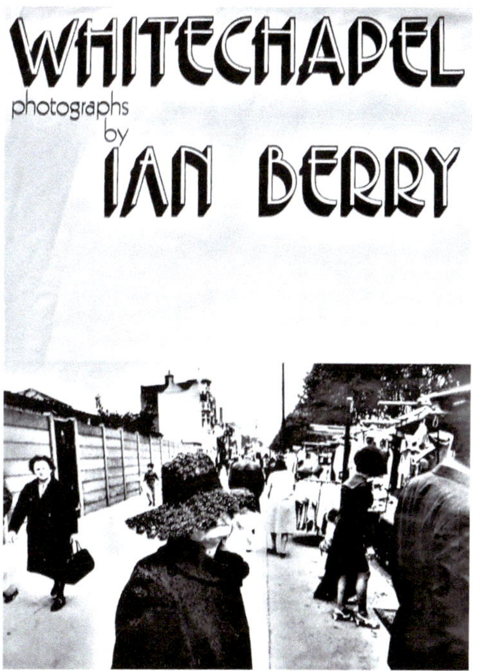

Ian Berry Photographer.

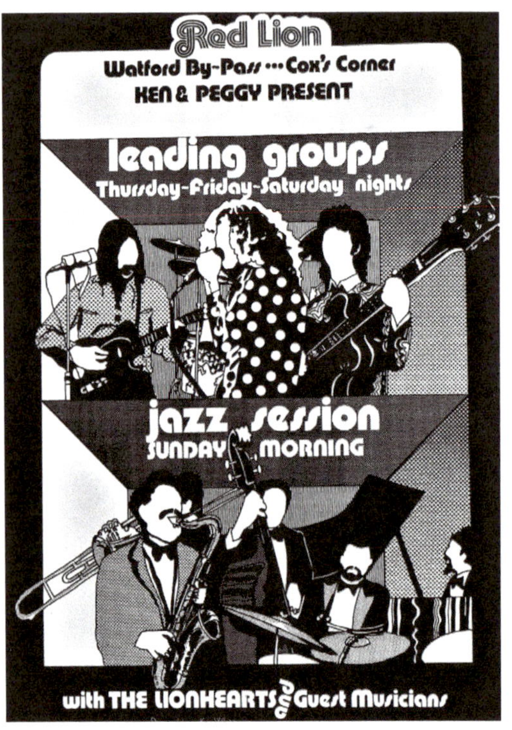

Fictional Jazz Pop Poster.

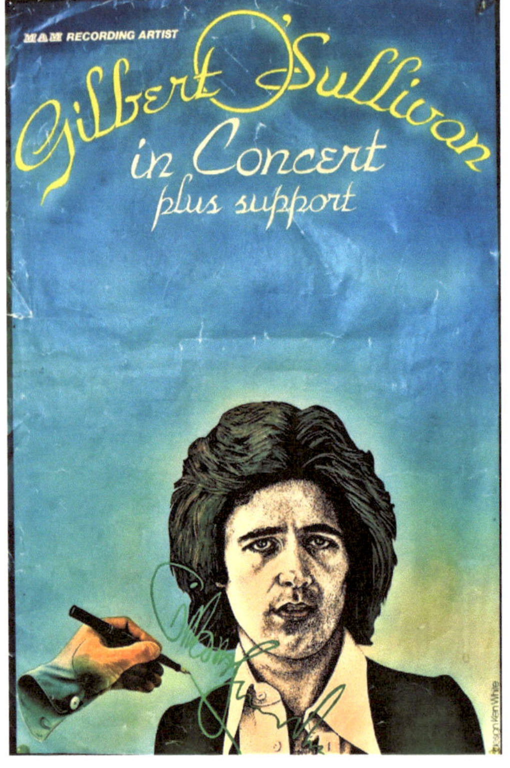

Gilbert O'Sullivan in concert.

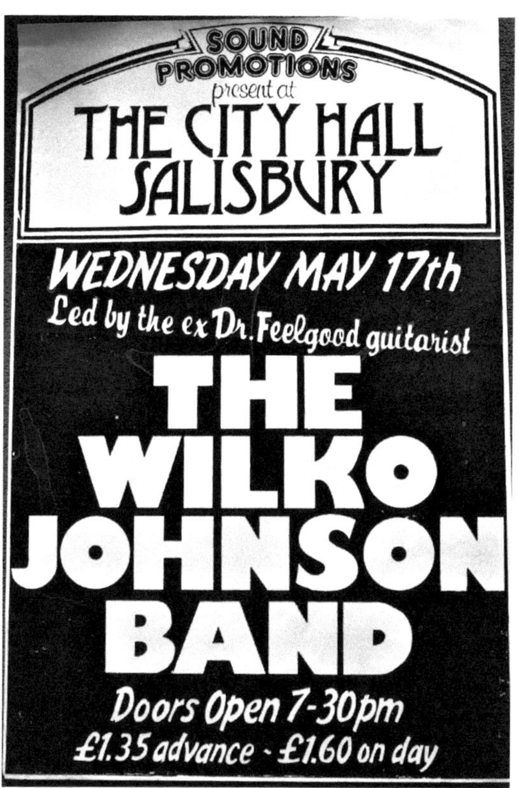

The Wilko Johnson Band at Salisbury.

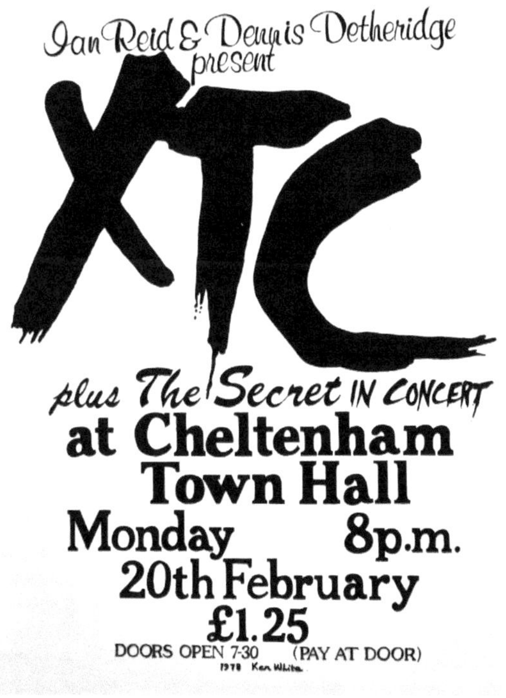

XTC at Cheltenham Town Hall.

The Swindon Murals

If the Golden Lion Bridge mural launched Ken into an international career in artistic sleight of hand, it was also the catalyst for controversy. Less concerned with Ken's means of creation or even the locations of the murals, arguments raged over who he put in them and why. Or not. A mural Ken painted for Swindon's Brunel Centre became a case in point, for no sooner did the voluptuous curves of Swindon-born actress Diana Dors appear on the wall than the work came to a shuddering halt. Cllr. Eammon Hackett attacked her inclusion, asserting that Miss Dors held no fondness for Swindon. Ergo, she didn't deserve to be in the mural. The chairman of the public works committee thus held up the painting proceedings until the committee had approved each of its component parts. Only then could Ken continue.

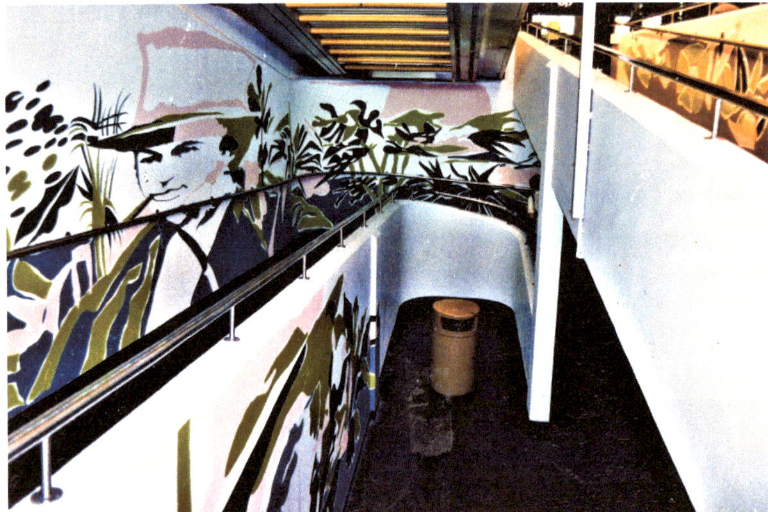

The Brunel Centre mural, *c.* 1984.

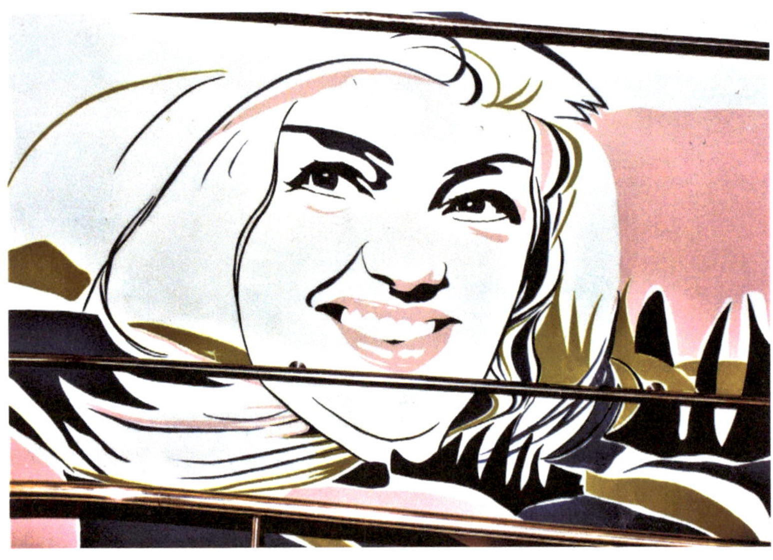

Swindon-born actor Diana Dors.

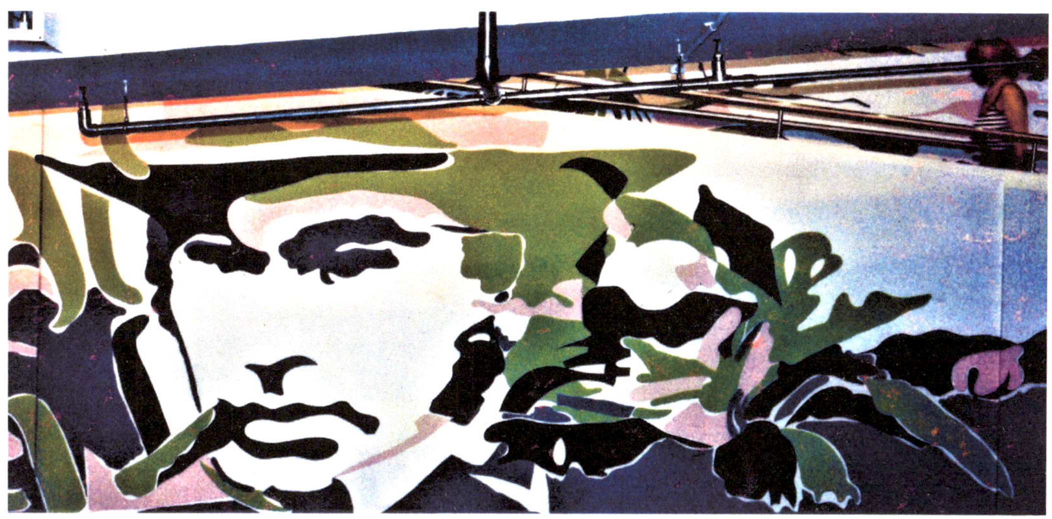

Isambard Kingdom Brunel – the father of New Swindon.

One of Ken's most-loved murals is his 1979 'shop front' featuring famous Swindonians, painted at the end of Union Street, in Old Town's Prospect Place. The mural depicted the shop as belonging to J. H. Jones – umbrella manufacturer. Peering from its windows, or arranged in front of it, were:

- Alf Brown – former mayor
- Bruce the collecting dog
- Isambard Kingdom Brunel
- Rick Davies – of Supertramp
- Diana Dors – actress, born in Swindon as Diana Fluck
- Harold Fleming – footballer, after whom Fleming Way is named
- John Francome – jockey
- Justin Hayward – pop artist
- Richard Jefferies – writer
- David Murray John – town clerk
- William Morris – founder of the *Swindon Advertiser* (not the wallpaper Morris)
- Gilbert O'Sullivan – singer/songwriter
- 'Raggy' Powell – philanthropic rag and bone dealer turned Alderman
- Don Rogers – Swindon Town footballer
- XTC pop group: Barry Andrews, Terry Chambers, Dave Gregory, Colin Moulding and Andy Partridge

Sad to say the owners of the house claimed that the mural caused damp in his house and so covered it over in 1991.

Despite Ken's murals appearing all over town, Swindon never gave him the level of carte blanche to his talent for the spectacular that secured his reputation on foreign shores.

A large Swindon piece often erroneously attributed to Ken once covered a car park wall, close to the railway station, to the east of the railway village between Fleet Street and Station Road. Sponsored by Arkell's Brewery, it depicted a King Class steam train

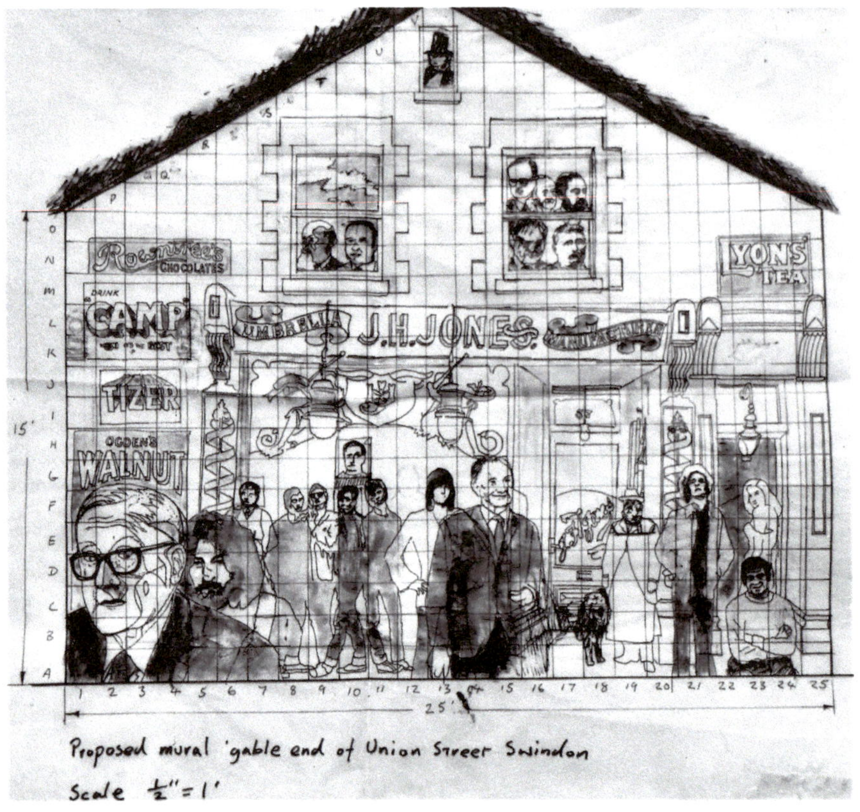

Ken's plan of the Swindon personalities mural was located in Prospect Place, Old Town. Ken painted this much-loved mural in 1979.

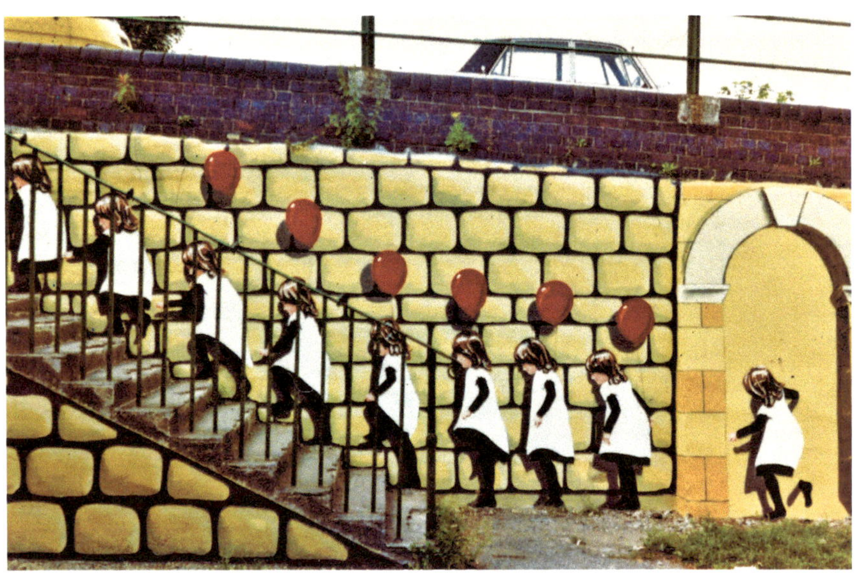

A section of Ken's Cambria Bridge mural, painted *c.* 1979..

thundering past the GWR Works. It was actually largely the work of Terry Court, aided and abetted by several youngsters on a job creation scheme, with minor tweaking by Ken when it was close to completion.

The 1970s and 1980s then was the heyday of Swindon's murals. Aside from the life-changing Golden Lion mural and the shop front, plus the locomotive described above, Ken's Swindon work also included a canal scene on Cambria Bridge Road beside the former Wilts & Berks Canal route, a mural in the Oasis leisure centre, body-builders in a gym, the out-of-town Cavendish Square shopping mall and an ocean liner at the nearby Highworth outdoor swimming pool painted in 1988. 30 feet high and complete with cruise liner passengers, this mural let swimmers imagine themselves diving into a pool on the deck of a luxury liner.

Pigs Might Fly? In Ken's World They Do!

We all know the adage about pigs not flying. Well in the image below, the Volunteer's Mural, they actually do! In a fabulous flight of fancy in this 1982 mural, celebrating fifty years of voluntary effort, one pig hangs out of a window and another seems to fly along the side of the building.

The central character in the doorway is Tom Fessey, who in the 1930s created Swindon's Council of Social Services. Looking out from the upstairs window are an ex-Mayor of Swindon, E. Millin and Gladys Plumley. When the *Swindon Advertiser* launched a Citizen of the Millennium poll in 1999, Gladys Plumley featured in the top ten. For nigh on thirty years, until fading eyesight forced retirement in 1970, Gladys had helped thousands of people seeking help at the Council for Social Services – later to become Swindon Voluntary Service Council.

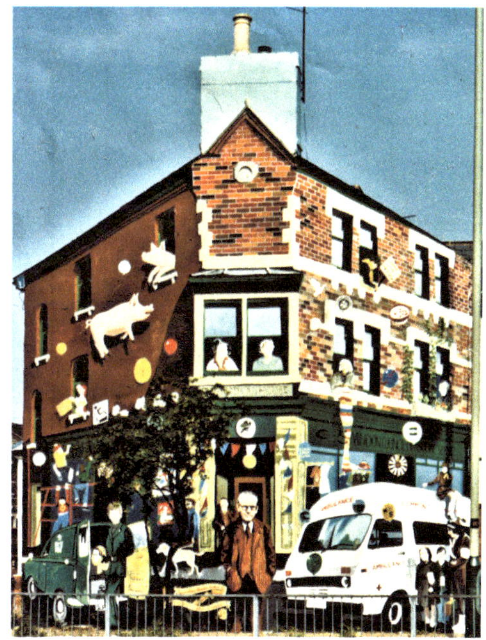

The Volunteer's mural on Iffley Road, *c*. 1982. This mural was painted with help from young, unemployed people.

NB: The rendering that eventually covered this Iffley Road mural is, at the time of writing, coming away in places, revealing tantalising glimpses of the mural.

In 1984, Ken showed a new facet to his wall-painting with a mural in a gym in London Street, in Swindon's Railway Village conservation area. Here, in a departure to anything he'd painted before or since, Ken had thirteen male and female bodybuilders rippling and flexing their way along 192 square feet of wall.

Later, in 1989, Ken turned Japanese with mural running along the corridors of the outpatient's department at the long-ago-demolished Princess Margaret Hospital. The finance for this work came from a grant from Southern Arts. It featured a linked set of images including a life-sized tiger stalking its way through bamboo trees, golden carp and a haiku.

Ken's brushes had a further jungle rumble a couple of years later for a setting at Richard Branson's twenty-first floor, Palm Beach nightclub.

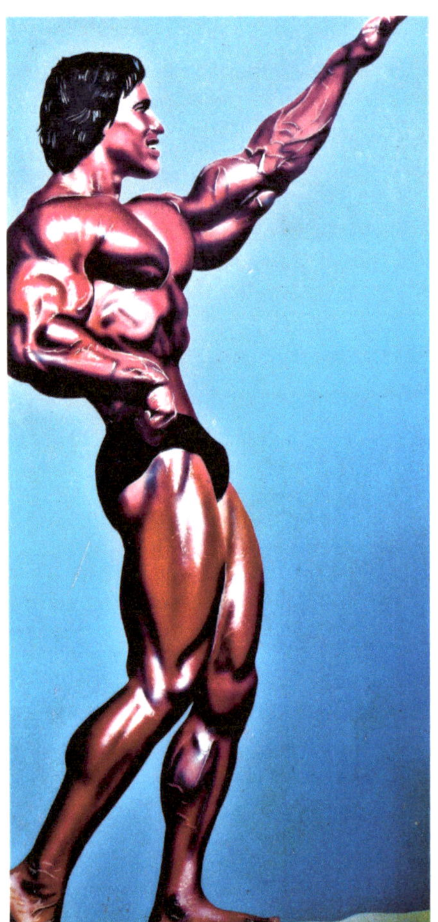 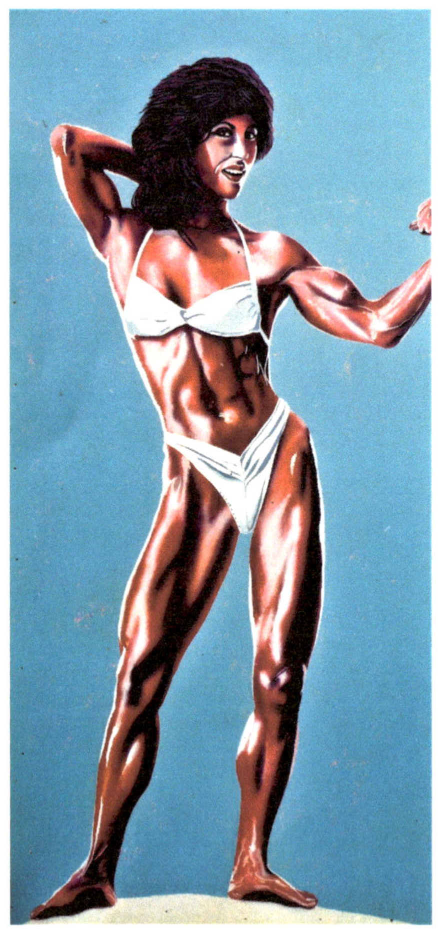

Above left: Bodybuilder mural – male form. 1984 mural for the Swindon Bodybuilder gym on London Road showing the weightlifters' stylized posturing.

Above right: Bodybuilder mural – female form.

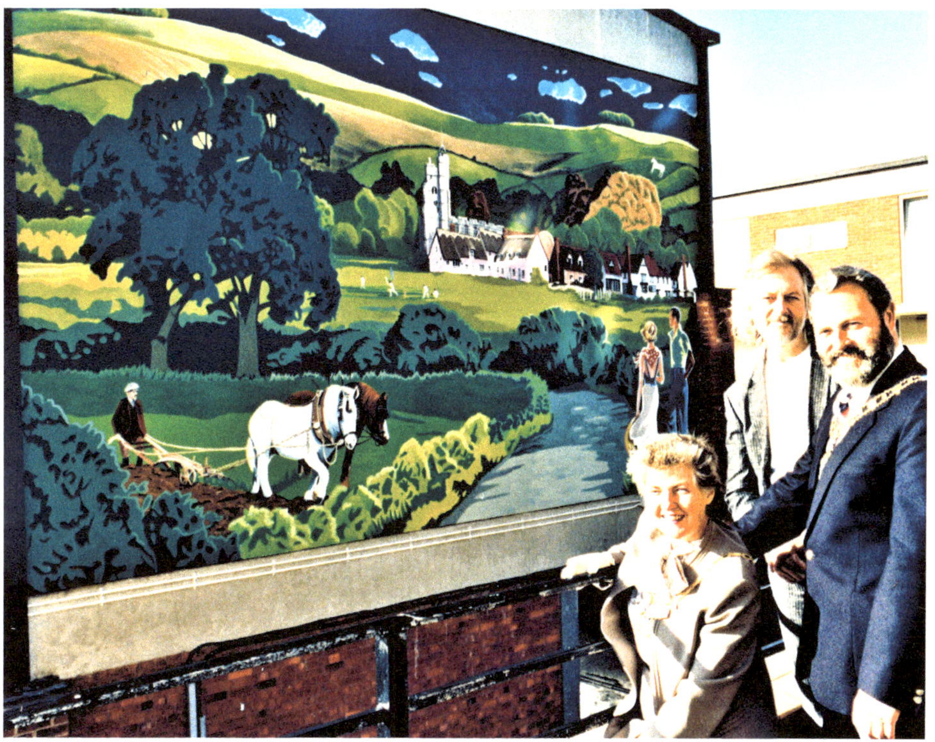

The Cavendish Square country scene mural, Walcot, Swindon, 1987. The mural depicts the village of Cavendish.

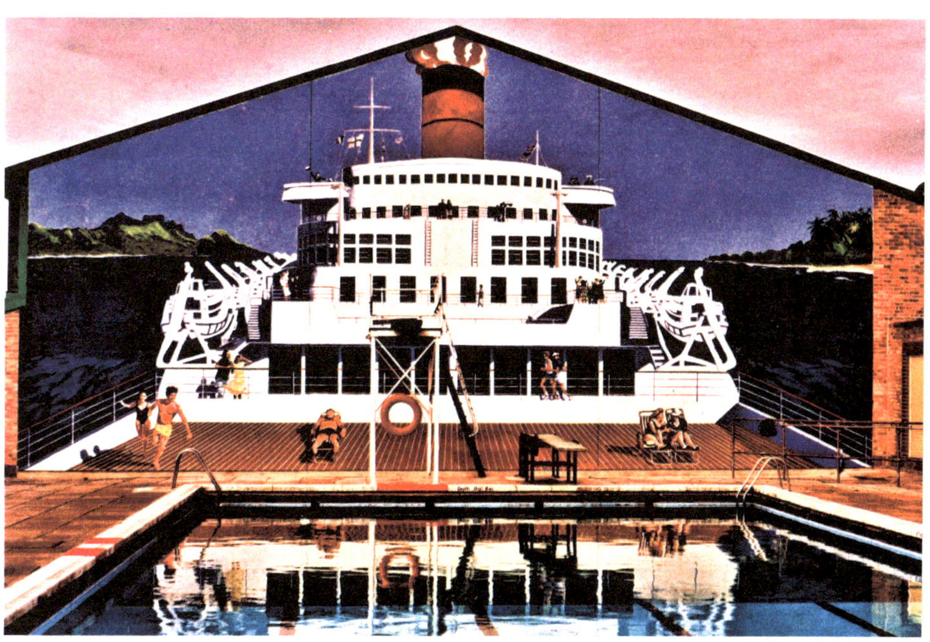

The cruise liner scene painted at Highworth Lido, 2008.

Chapter 3

Other UK Murals

The Scottish Murals

Controversy around Ken's work didn't restrict itself to Swindon. 1983 saw Ken invited north of the border, to paint a mural on a wall in a new shopping complex in the Fife town of Kirkcaldy. But a Scottish storm blew up around his work when he painted Kirkcaldy-born Jocky Wilson, the champion darts player, into a swimming pool scene. He also placed a local councillor and a 'Mr Nobody' into the mural – this anonymous man wearing a bowler hat and gripping a brolly is a recurrent motif in Ken's mural work.

In similar fashion to the Swindon shenanigans around Diana Dors et al, the Kirkcaldy council found reasons to object to each of the portraits. They wanted them replacing with likenesses of deceased local worthies. Hence, Ken had to overpaint the councillor and the dart's player with the explorer John McDouall Stuart. As for Mr Nobody though, they granted him permission to remain when Ken explained he represented a drowning Englishman!

Elsewhere in Scotland, on a commission from the Scottish Arts Council, Ken painted a 3,000-square-foot Victorian elevation on the brick walls of the Smith & Wellstood Columbia stoveworks – a Bonnybridge iron foundry. He painted Smith and Wellstood standing in front of the building with some of the workers looking out of its windows. For this work Ken won the prestigious Saltire Society Arts and Crafts in Architecture Awards for 1981. Sadly, three years later the premises closed and the buildings were demolished. Take note Swindonians: not only in your town.

In 2004 the Royal National Lifeboat Museum, together with a community group, the Off the Wall Project, engaged themselves in efforts to establish a heritage mural trail at Invergordon on Scotland's Cromarty Forth. They wanted the murals to form part of the town's regeneration, with the aim of encouraging tourists disembarking from cruise ships to spend time in the town instead of, as was usual, simply passing through en route to Loch Ness.

For them Ken created three large murals:

1. The 640-square-foot loch scene inspired by the Kildary Angling club who fished the waters there.

2. *The Volunteer Spirit* – an RNLI lifeboat
3. A depiction of a 1800s Saltburn street scene. This he presented as a triptych in the High Street on the gable end of a rough-stoned terrace and the building next to it at right angles.

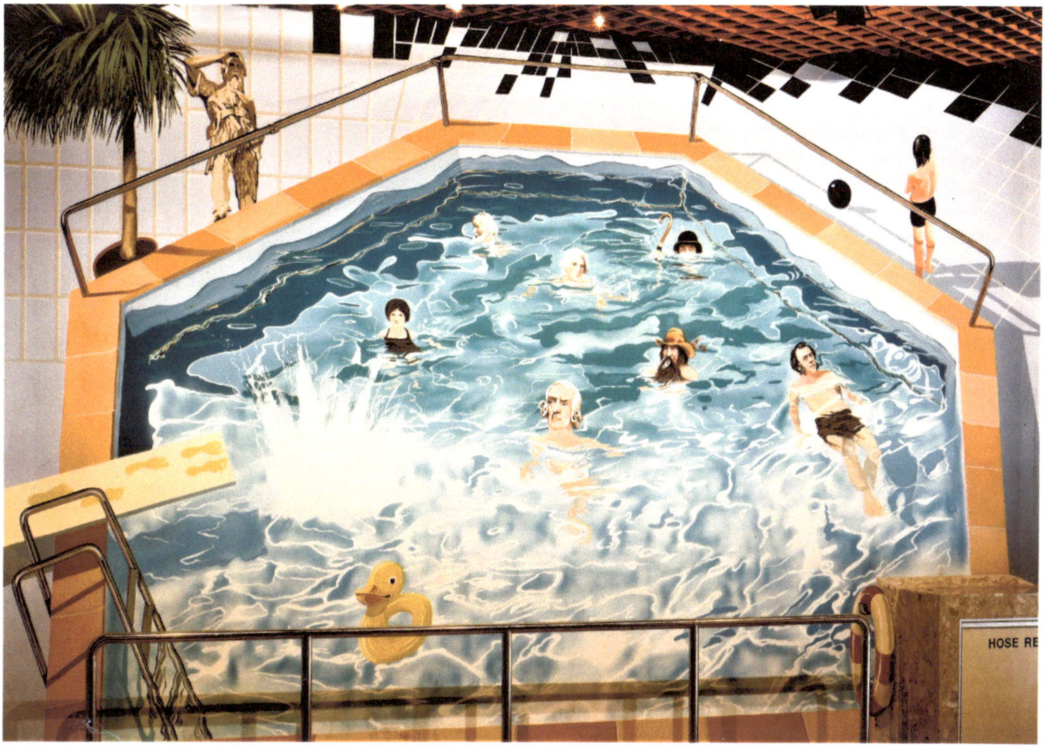

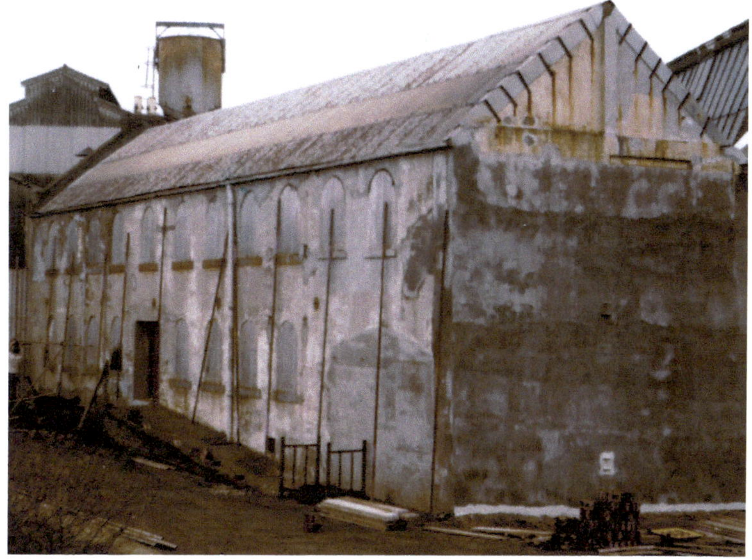

Above: Kirkcaldy Shopping Centre (Mercat) mural, 1983.

Right: The Smith & Wellstood building in Bonnybridge, Scotland, before Ken began work on it, 1980.

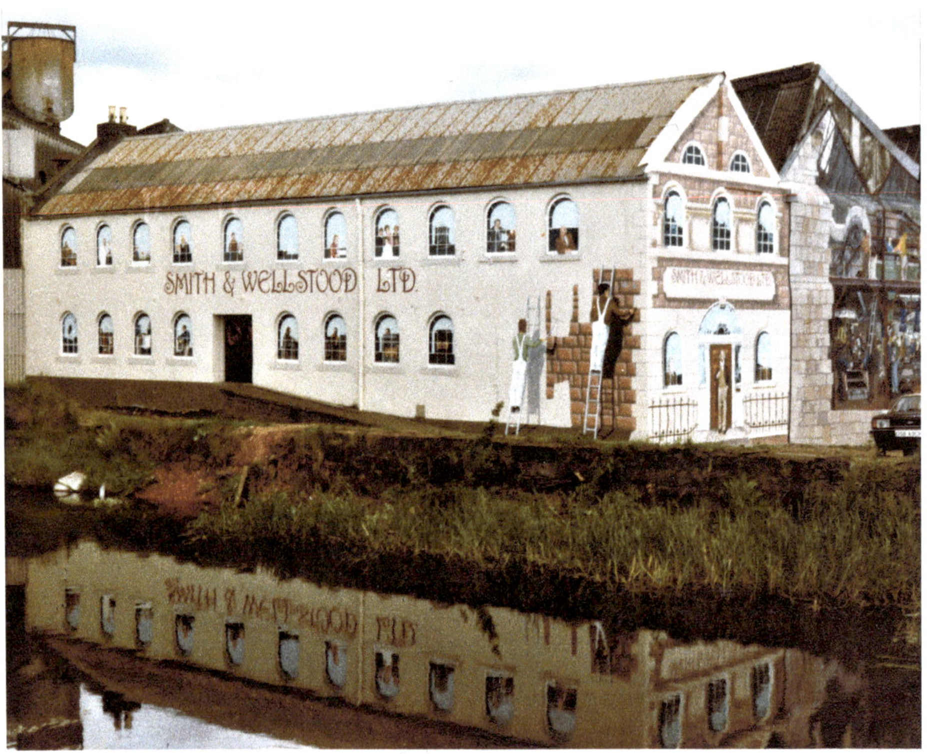

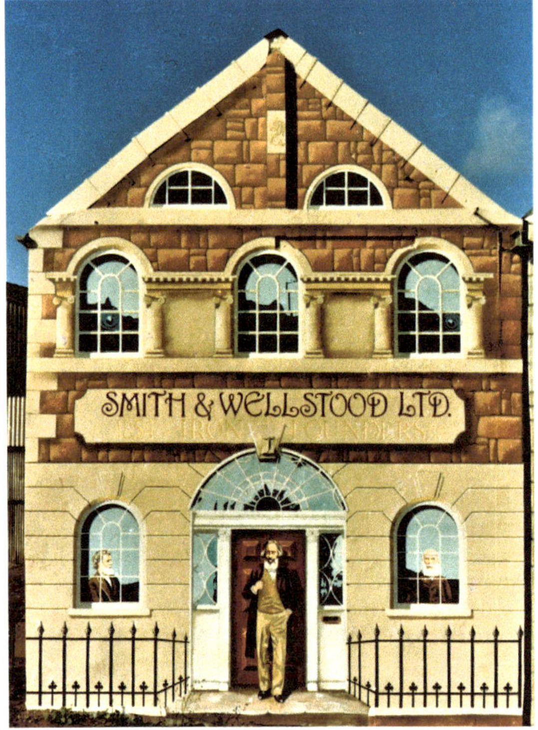

Above: The Smith & Wellstood
building: side and main elevation.

Left: The Smith & Wellstood
building: front elevation.

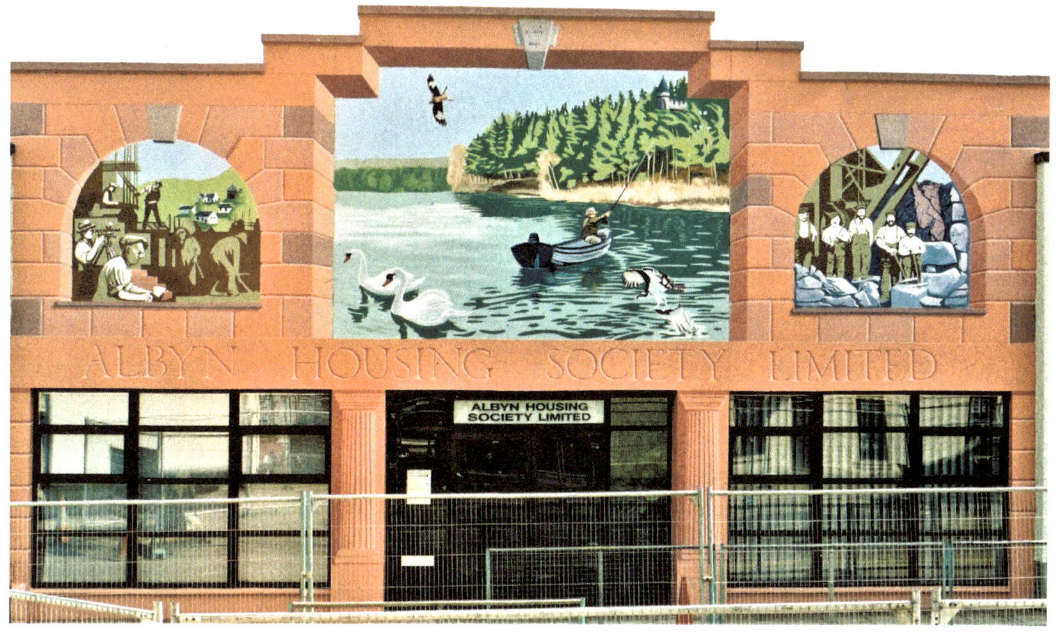

Above: The Loch scene at Invergordon, Scotland, 2004.

Right: The Lifeboat at Invergordon, Scotland, 2005.

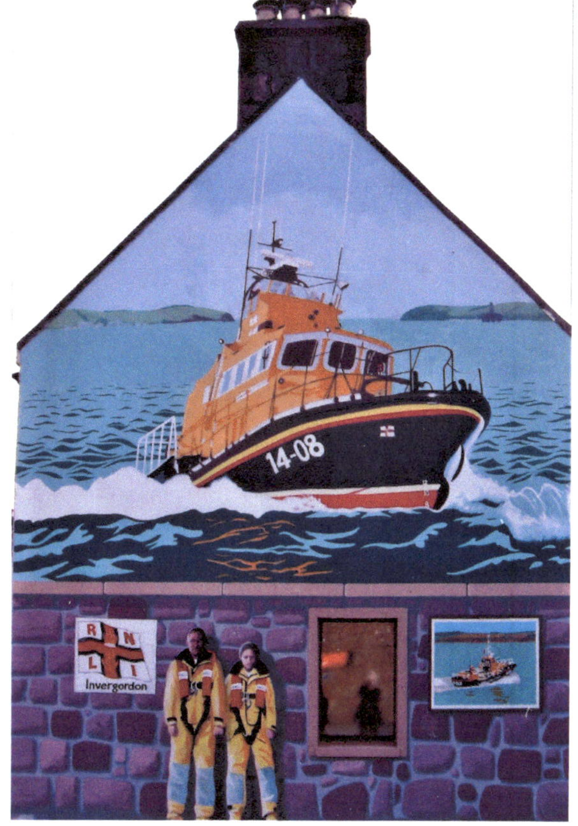

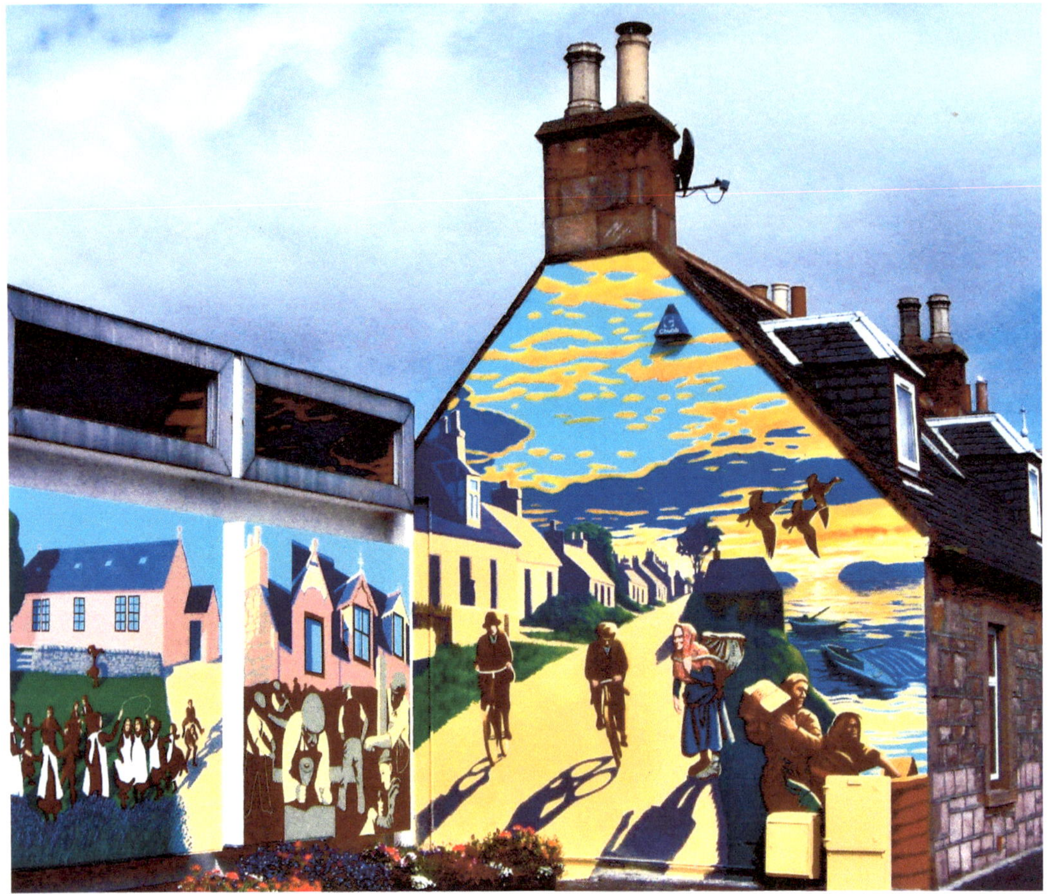

The Saltburn Street scene, Scotland, 2007.

London Murals

Back on the English side of that long, meandering wall built by Hadrian, in London Ken was well-occupied. In the period between 1984 and 2004, his paintbrushes busied themselves on a range of exterior and interior walls. This book's beginning alluded to some of them.

One such was the faux Georgian, Covent Garden townhouse commissioned by Jacob Rothschild. Yet another was a scene from the Battle of Trafalgar at The Gun – an eighteenth-century Grade II listed pub in London's Coldharbour, in the Docklands. The mural depicts Admiral Horatio Nelson preparing to do battle with the French. The pub's landlord stands beside him and they're both wearing the naval attire of the period.

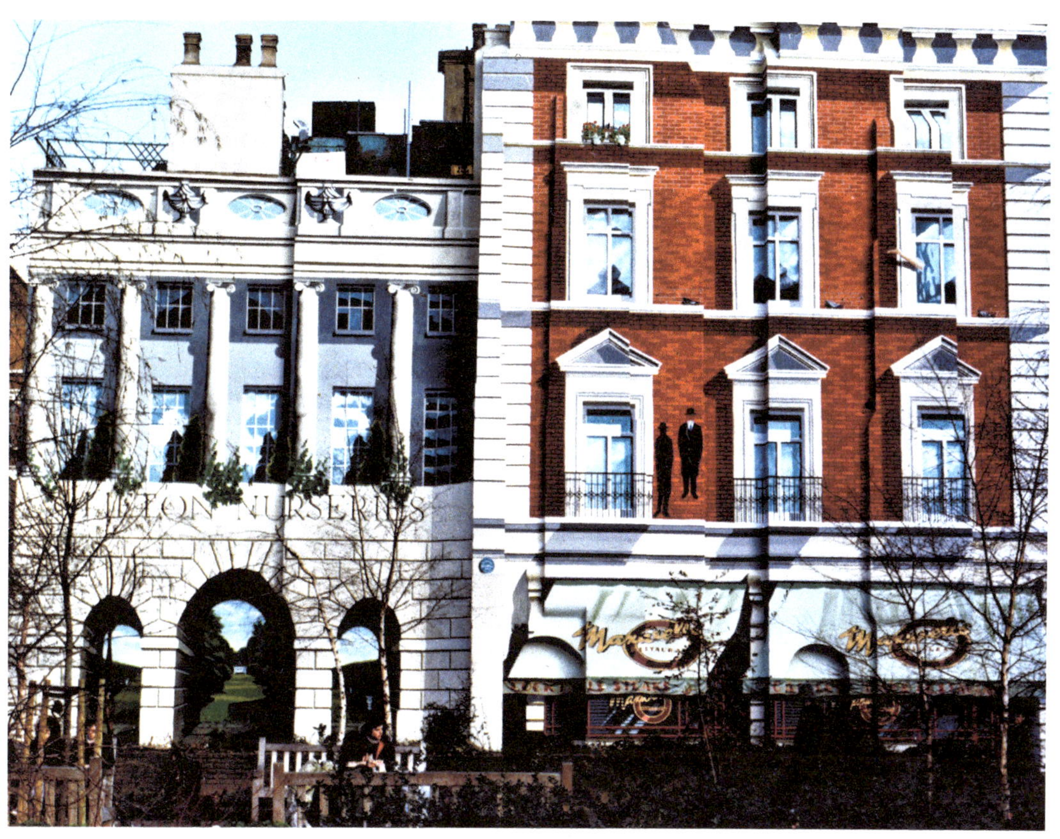

Covent Garden after painting.

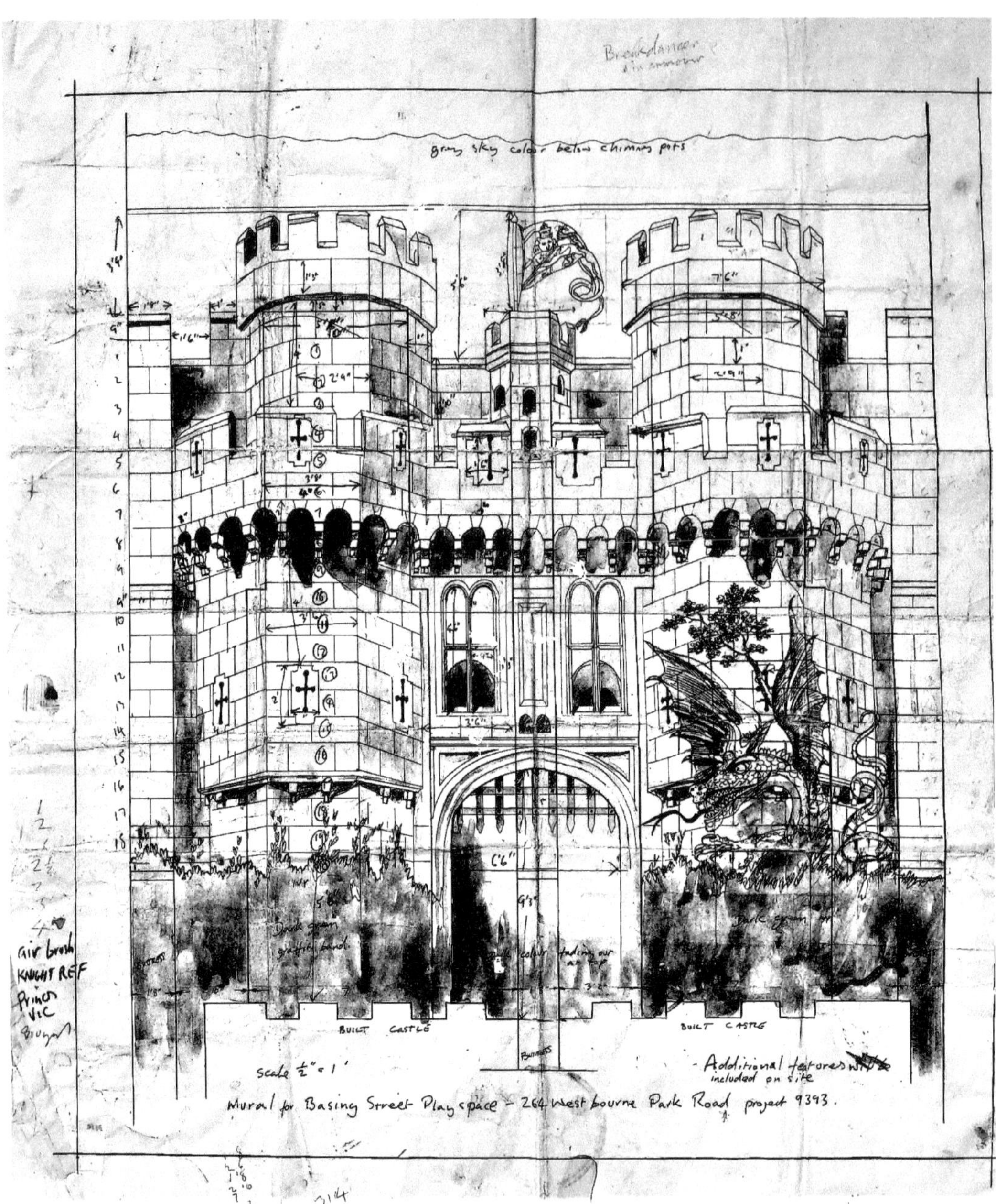

The castle plans.

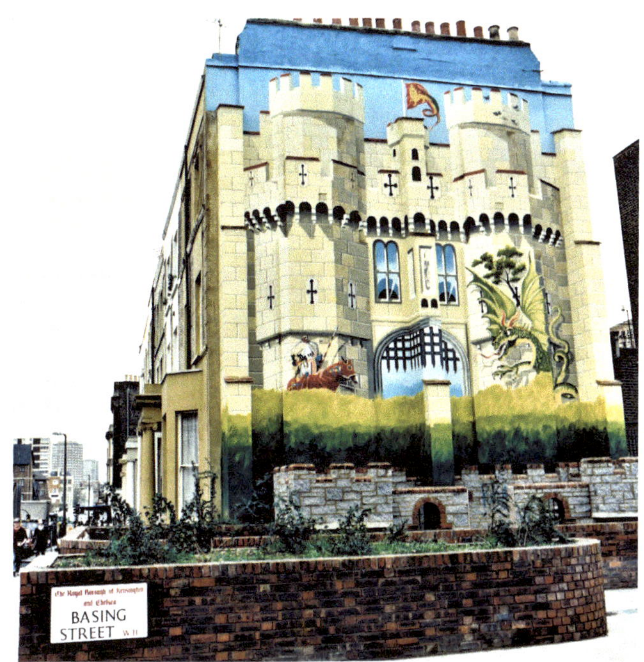

The castle mural at Basing Street, London, 1984.

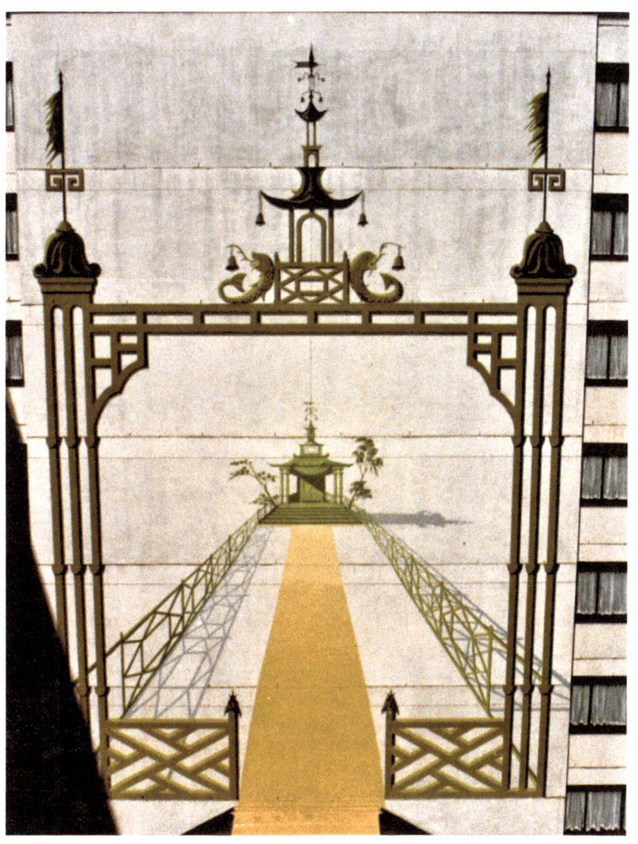

Intercontinental Hotel, London, 1985.

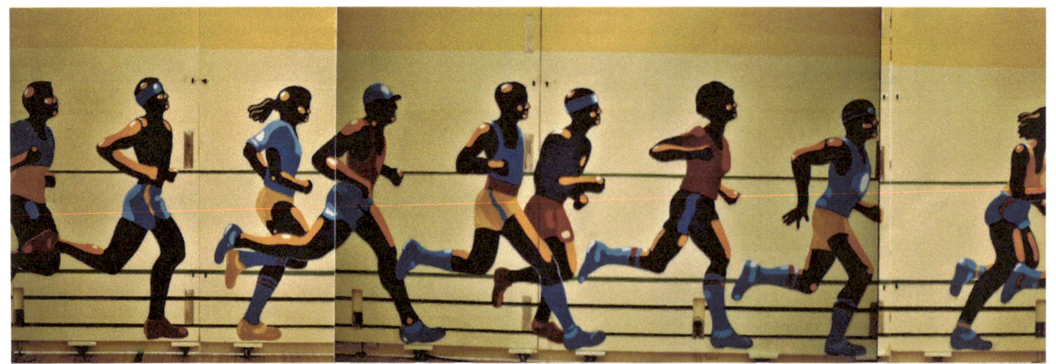

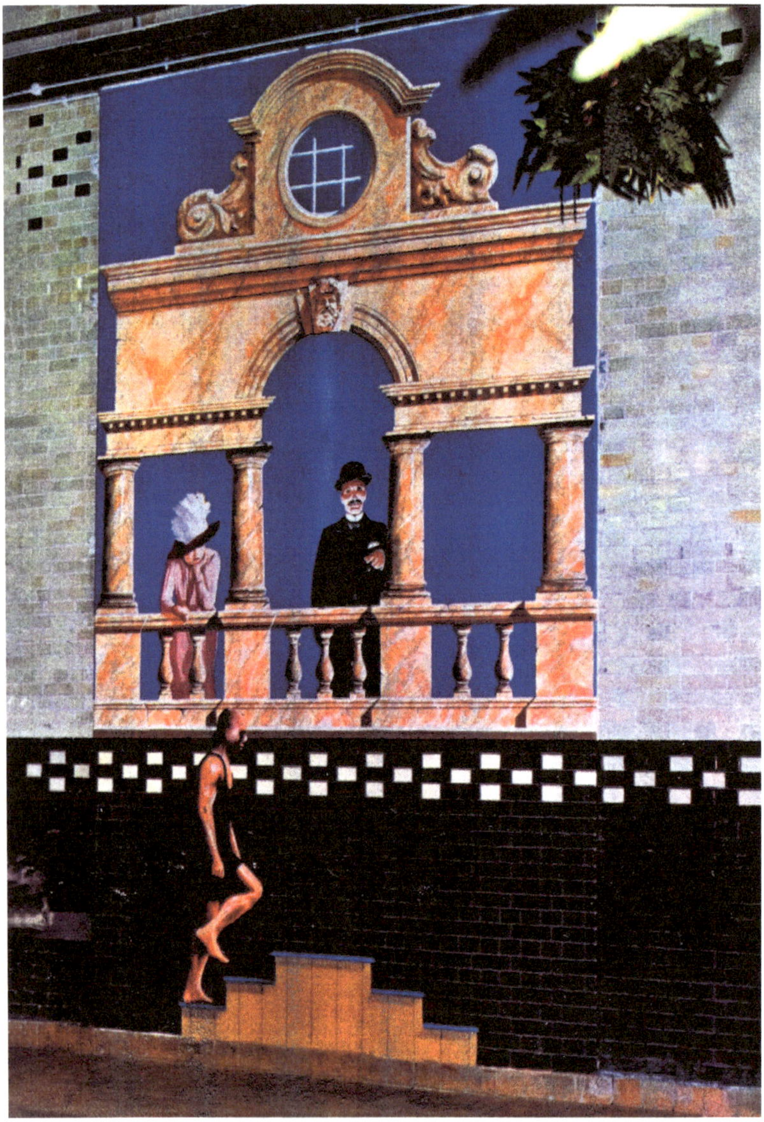

Above and left: Kensington and Chelsea swimming pool, 1989.

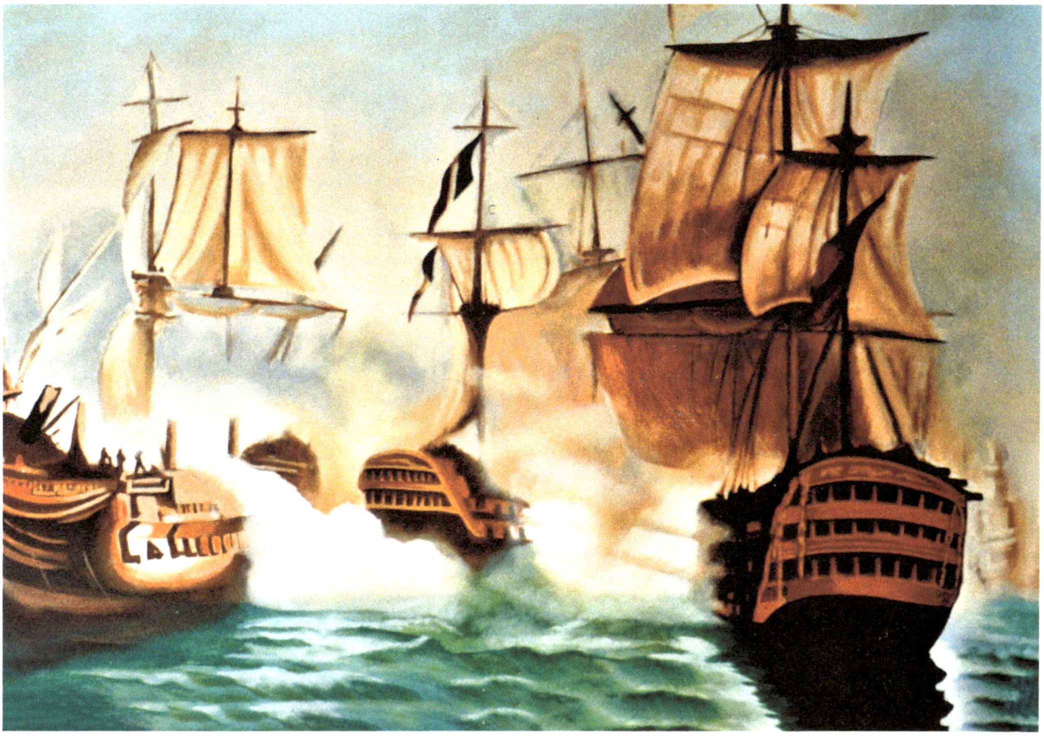

Above and below: The Gun public house, London, 2004.

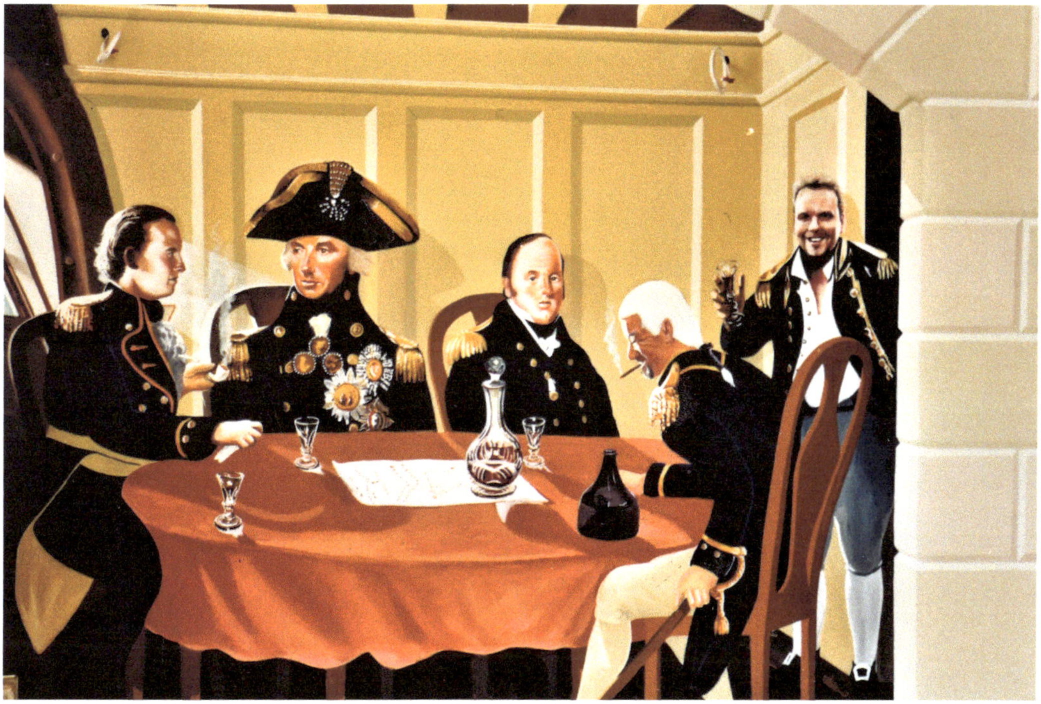

Other UK Murals

In 1983, and even closer to home than London, Ken donned his metaphorical pith helmet to return to the jungle yet again. This time the commission came from multi-millionaire financier Alex Burbage to paint a jungle scene in a room at Sutton Manor, Nr Winchester. No doubt it was a roaring success.

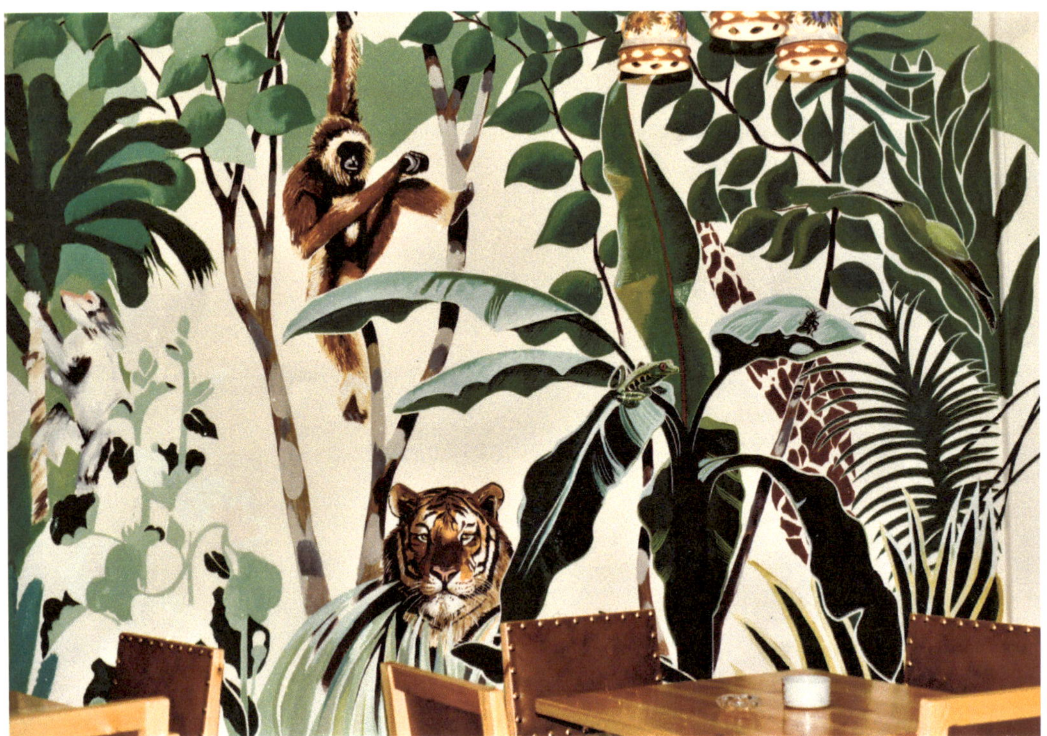

The Sutton Manor mural, Scotney, Hants.

Returning to the naval theme – well a naval location at least – controversy once more dogged Ken's brushstrokes, this time in Plymouth in 2002. Carrying out a commission for Plymouth City Council, Ken became dragged into a political row. With an impressive 40-foot feat of *Trompe-l'œil*, representing a three-storey Georgian town-house façade complete with classical pillars and open balustrade, Ken transformed an unattractive concrete gable end of a terraced property. But the national housing charity Shelter were outraged. They claimed that the money could and should have been better spent on buying two properties to house the homeless. Quick to leap on the bandwagon, Conservative council members described the project as a 'loony waste of money'. And a petty political war of words followed.

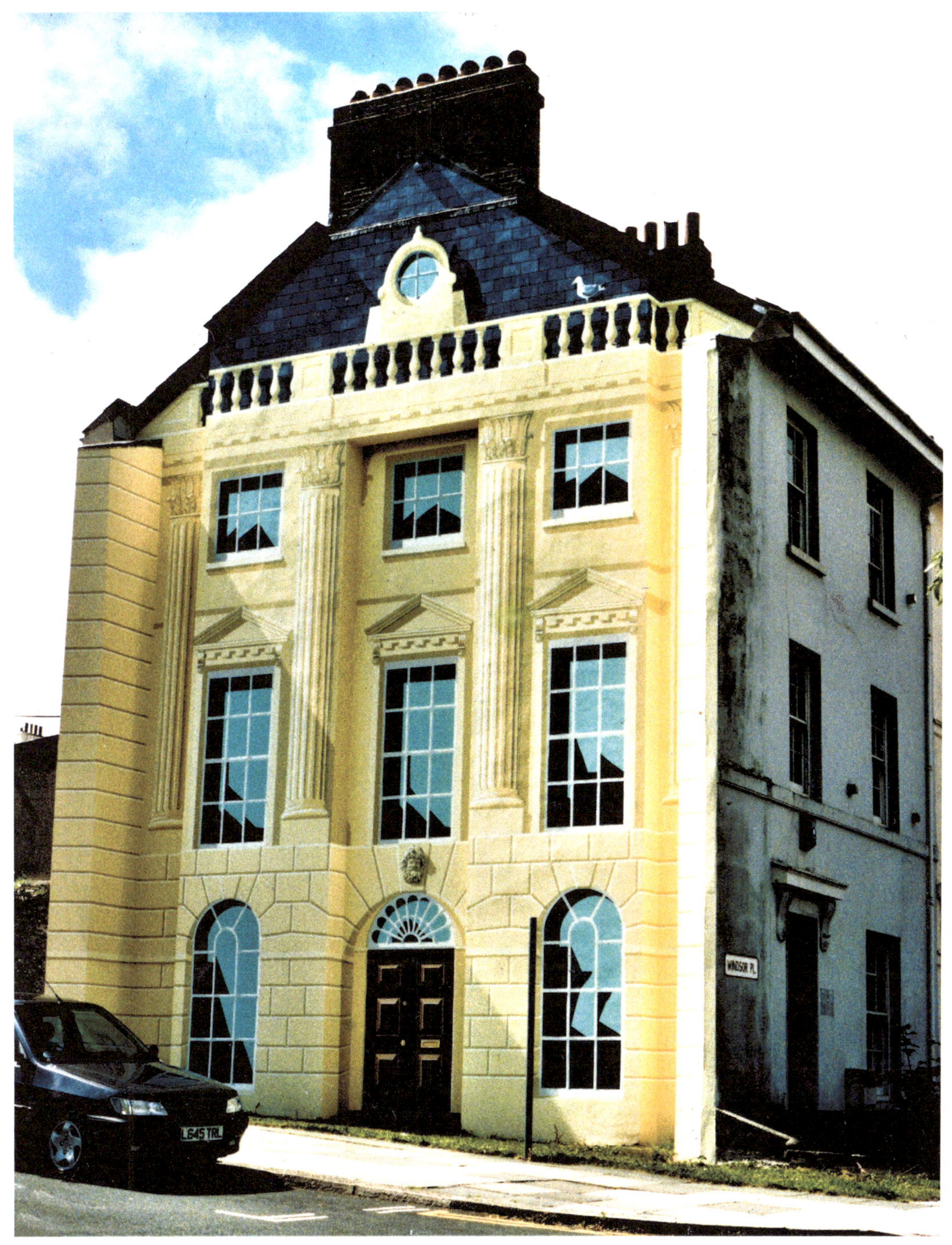

The Plymouth Town House mural, 1978.

Chapter 4

The Virgin Years

In 1968, when aged sixteen, Richard Branson first dipped his toe into publishing, via a magazine entitled *Student*. As an aspiring artist, the young Ken, touting his folder of work around, approached the magazine with a drawing of the entertainer Dudley Moore. Though successful in this endeavour, this wasn't the catalyst for the longstanding Branson/White relationship. That came a decade or thereabouts later.

Ken Gets Noticed

Bayer's 1977 decision to use Ken's Golden Lion mural in their large-scale advertising campaign proved to be crucial for Ken, for it led to one Richard Branson sitting up and taking notice. Or one of Branson's staff at least – they saw it and brought it to the boss's attention.

The artist and the work were duly noted and filed away by Branson, for when such a time arose as he could use Ken's undoubted talents. Such an opportunity came not much later, in 1978, when he moved into his Shepherd's Bush Town House recording studios. On a freelance basis, Branson employed Ken to paint the mural you see in the following images.

The back of the building featured the illusion of glass in the upper window shattering from the inside and cascading down in front of the window below. These windows, a permanent dazzling blue in an eternal sunlight, were a clever emulsion façade.

On the heels of this first freelance commission from Branson came three more, including the Sex Pistols' *The Great Rock 'n Roll Swindle* in London's Shepherd's Bush, and, also in Shepherd's Bush, a promotional mural for Mike Oldfield's *Incantations*.

It took until 1984 for Branson to place Ken on a life-transforming retainer with a sign for the Victoria pub in Uxbridge, London. It almost didn't happen though. In that year, Ken was busy painting the Blitz at Cornwall's no-longer-existing Aero Park, near Helston, when he got a call from the Virgin boss offering him a further commission. Ken, busy with the Blitz, turned him down and Branson had to engage another artist, who it seems made a poor job of it. So Branson returned to Ken as soon as he became available. Thus began a twenty-year relationship that sent Ken around the world to a variety of exotic locations. What's more it afforded him and his family financial security and Ken the opportunity to do other work, on the proviso that if Branson called Ken dropped what he was doing and went.

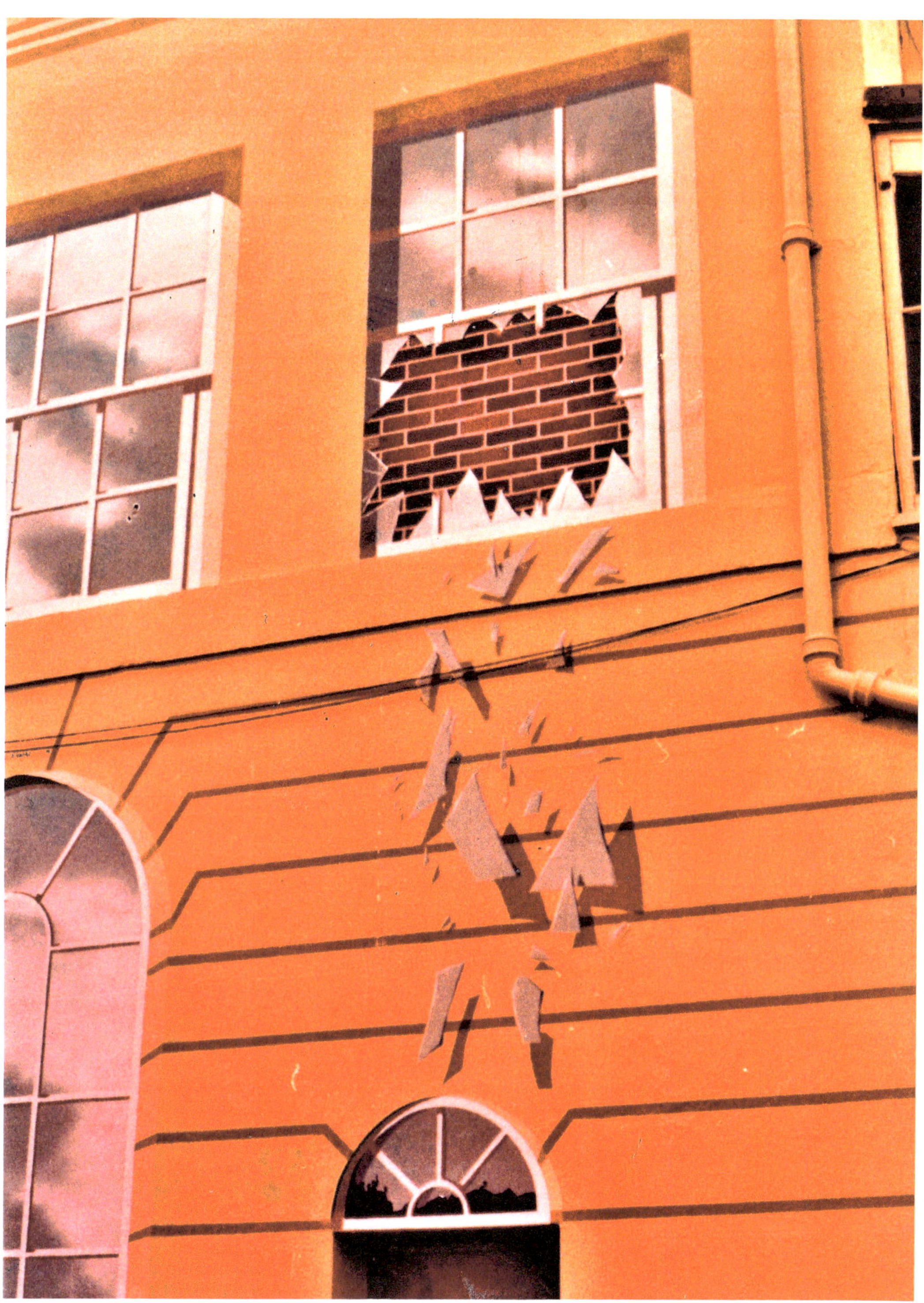

The Town House, London – broken glass.

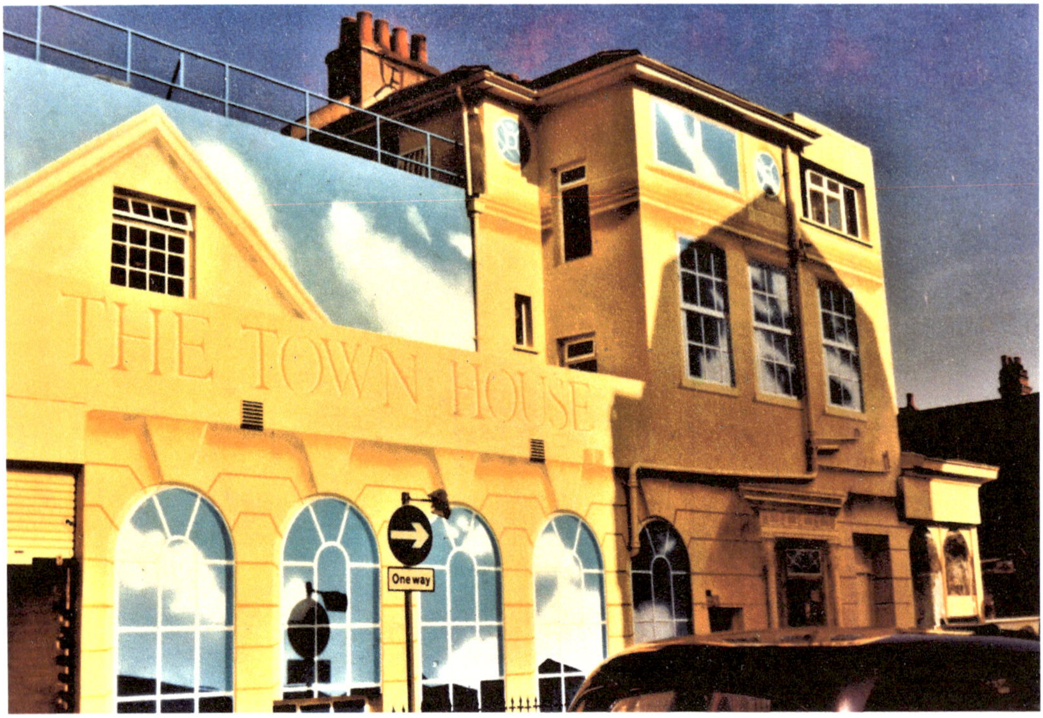

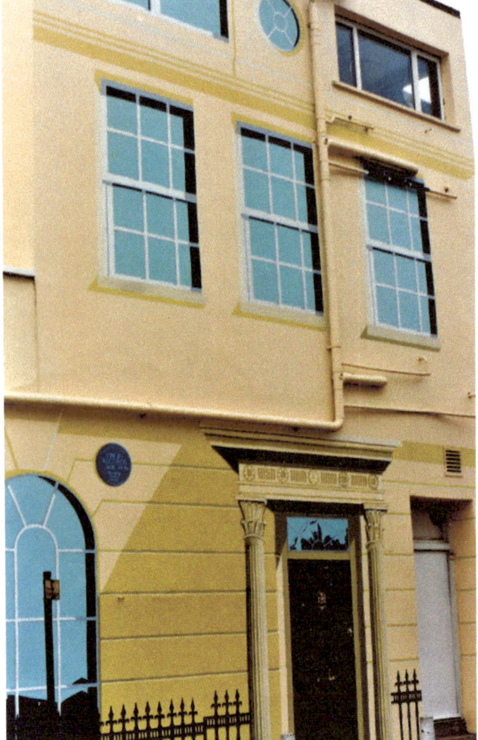

Above: The Town House, London – front elevation.

Left: The Town House, Goldhawk Road, London, 1978.

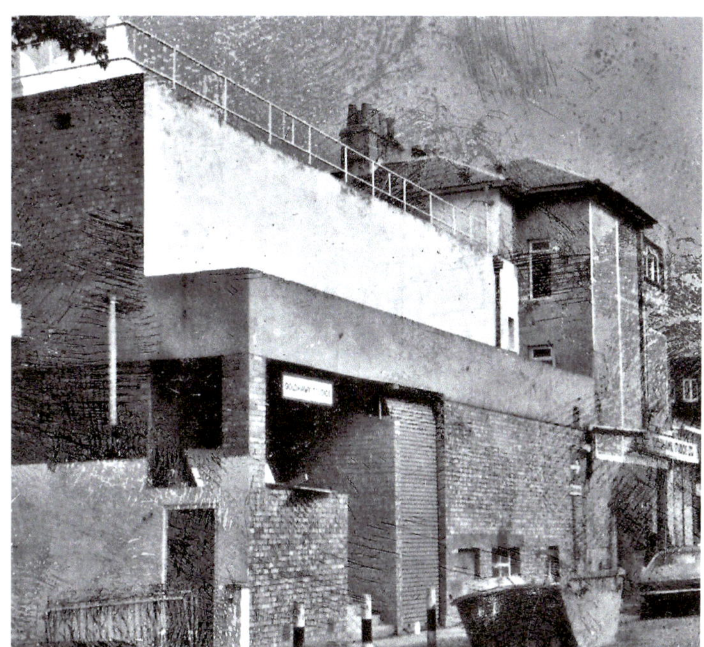

The Town House before Ken's treatment.

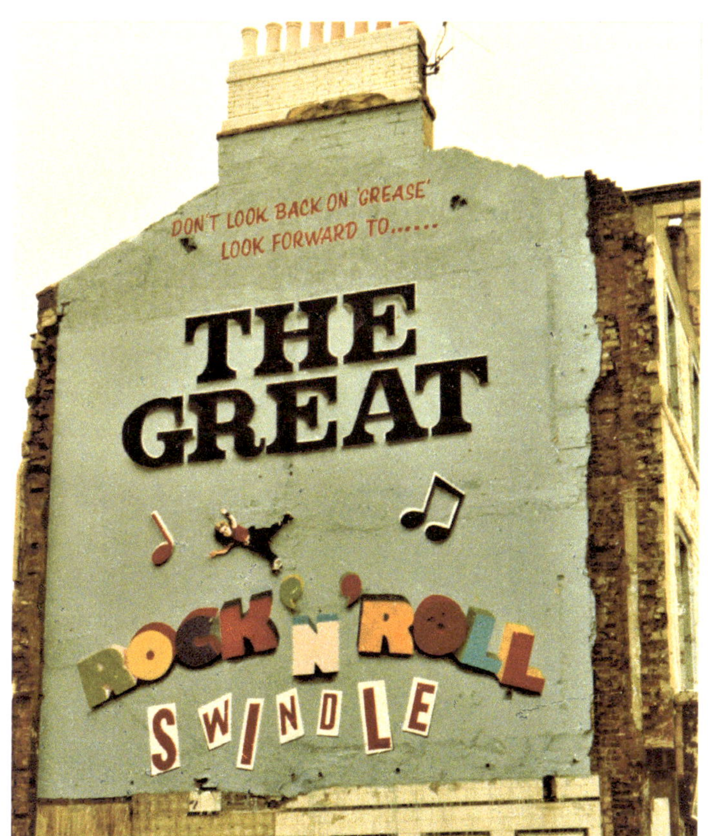

The Sex Pistols' *Great Rock 'n' Roll Swindle*, 1979.

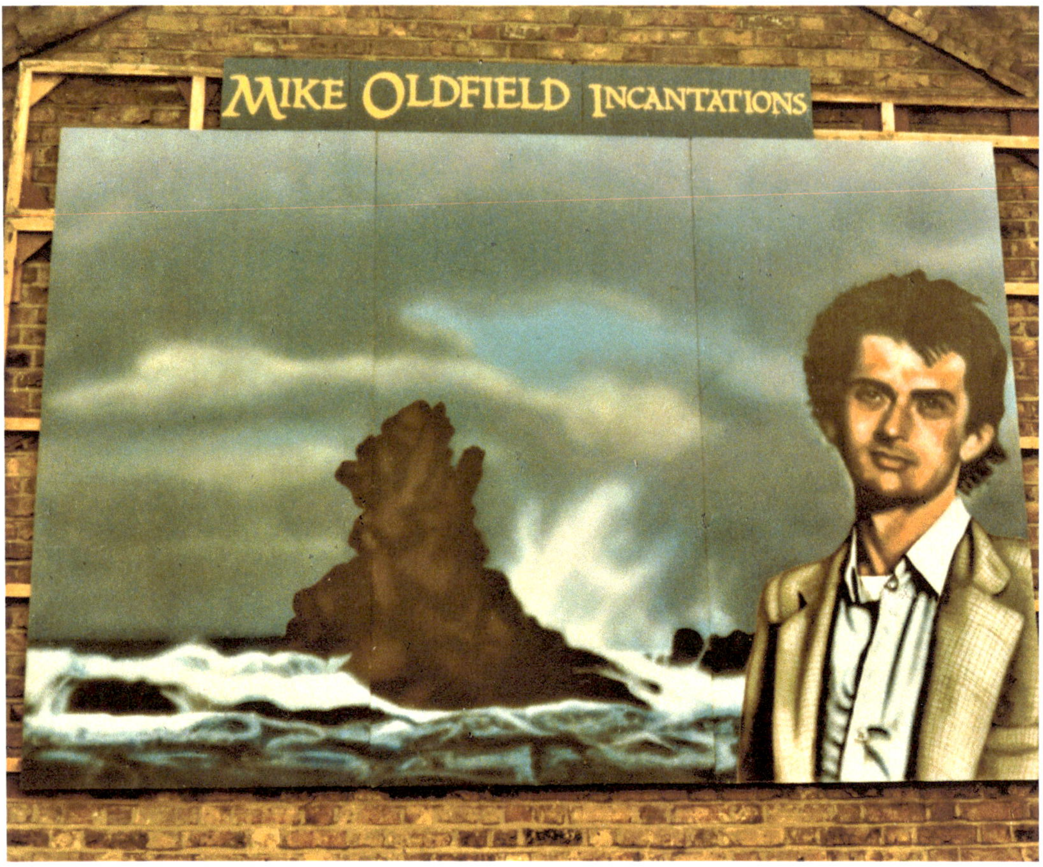

Mike Oldfield's *Incantations*, Shepherd's Bush, 1979.

From Oxfordshire to Orange County

It started then with the London Town House. Then came murals on Branson's homes in Kidlington, Oxfordshire and Palm Beach, Florida. One of these commissions included a set of Disney characters for Branson's children.

From there, Ken painted a variety of murals in Virgin offices, hotels and megastores across the globe.

Ken White's artistry has brushed landscapes and characters across surfaces in Amsterdam, Bergamo, Frankfurt, Los Angeles, Maastricht, Madrid, Majorca, Malaga, Milan, New Jersey, Salzburg, Vienna and Vigo. In all cases Ken had a free hand and a blank canvas in every sense. Branson's briefings tended to verge on the minimalist: 'There's a wall. Paint it.' Ken's response to that was to make the mural fit the location. Thus, Brussels got Magritte and Los Angeles got famous film stars – and so on.

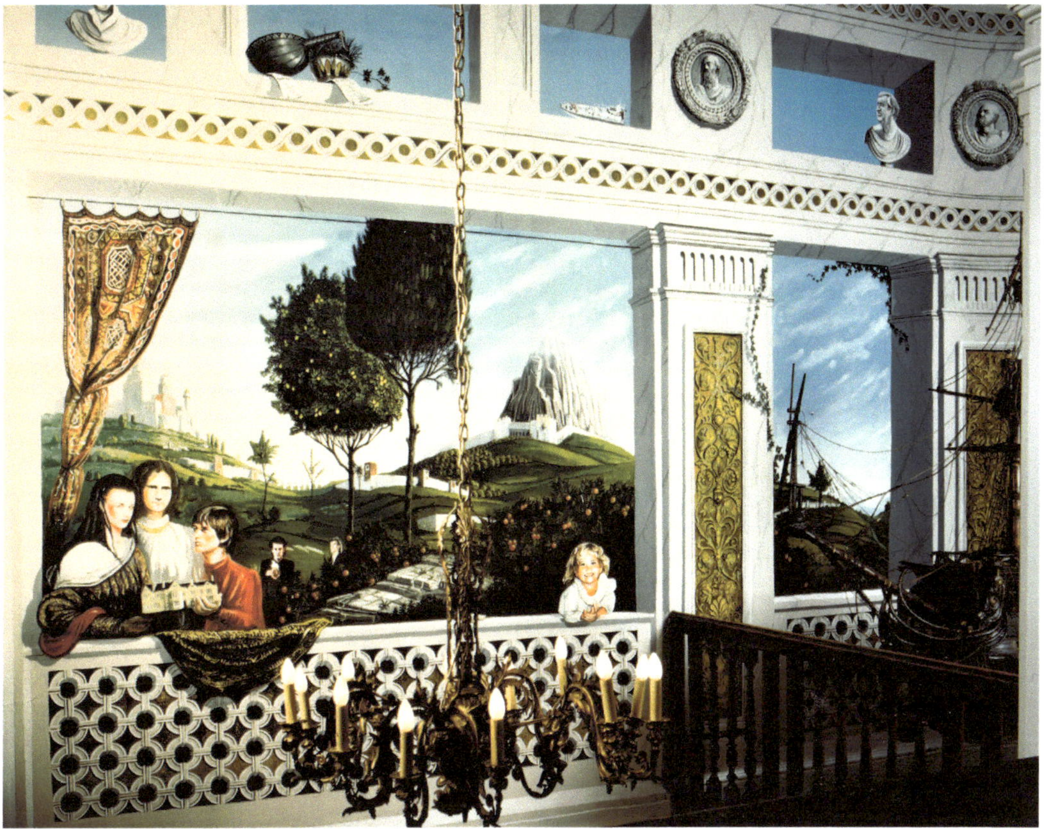

The Manor, Kidlington, Oxford, 1986.

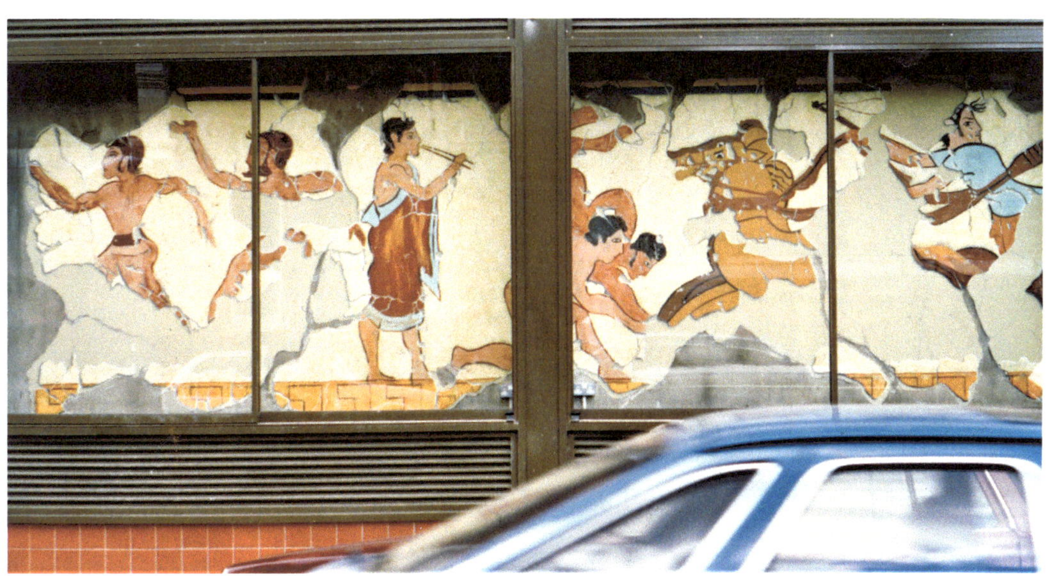

Olympic Studios, London.

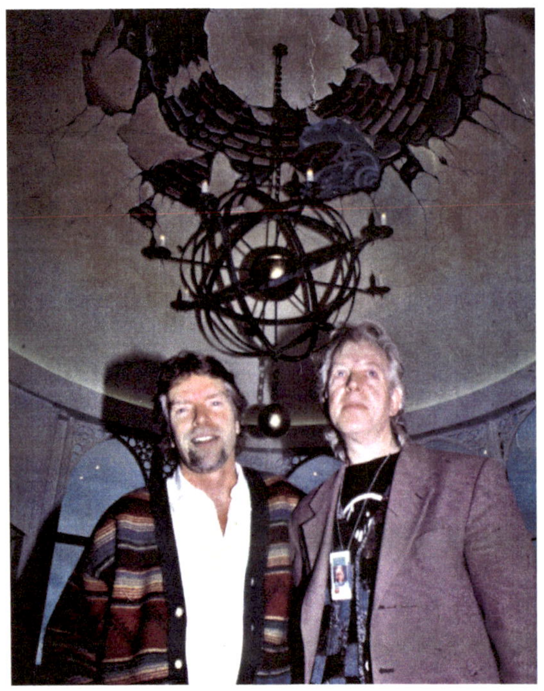

Ken with Richard Branson.

Virgin Shops and Restaurants: Europe

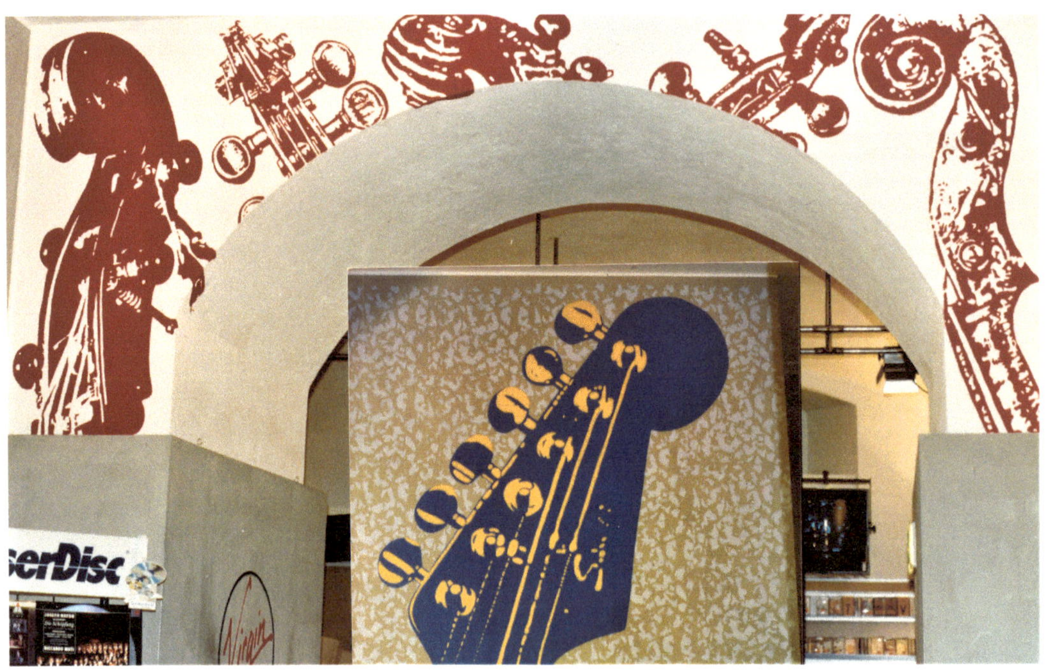

Milan Virgin megastore, 1992.

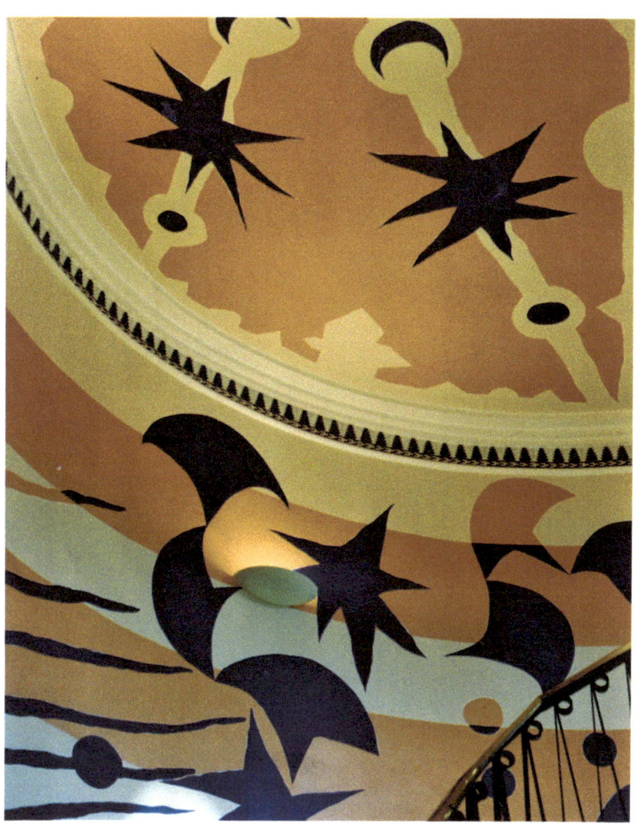

Seville Virgin megastore, 1995.

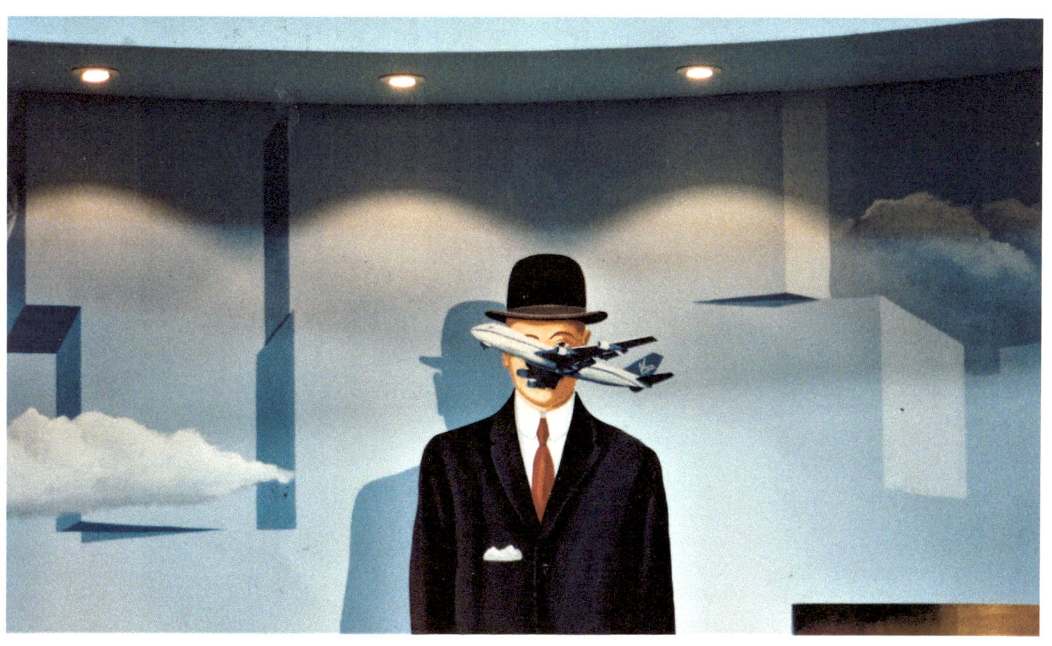

Brussels Virgin megastore, 1995.

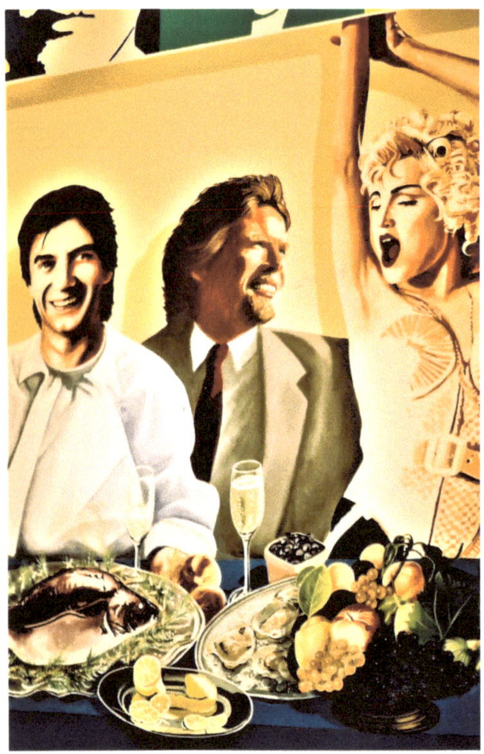

Left: La Petit Blanc restaurant, 2001.

Below: Ken White creating a mural of The Beatles in the Virgin XS store, Liverpool, 1997.

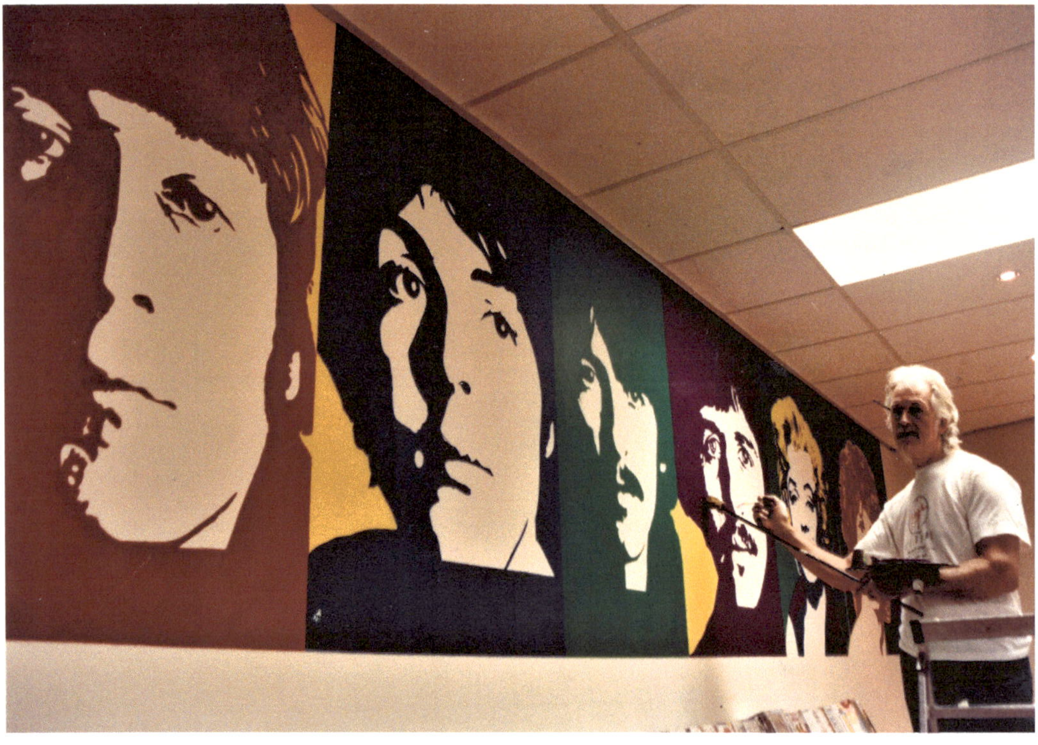

Virgin Shops, Restaurants and Others: USA

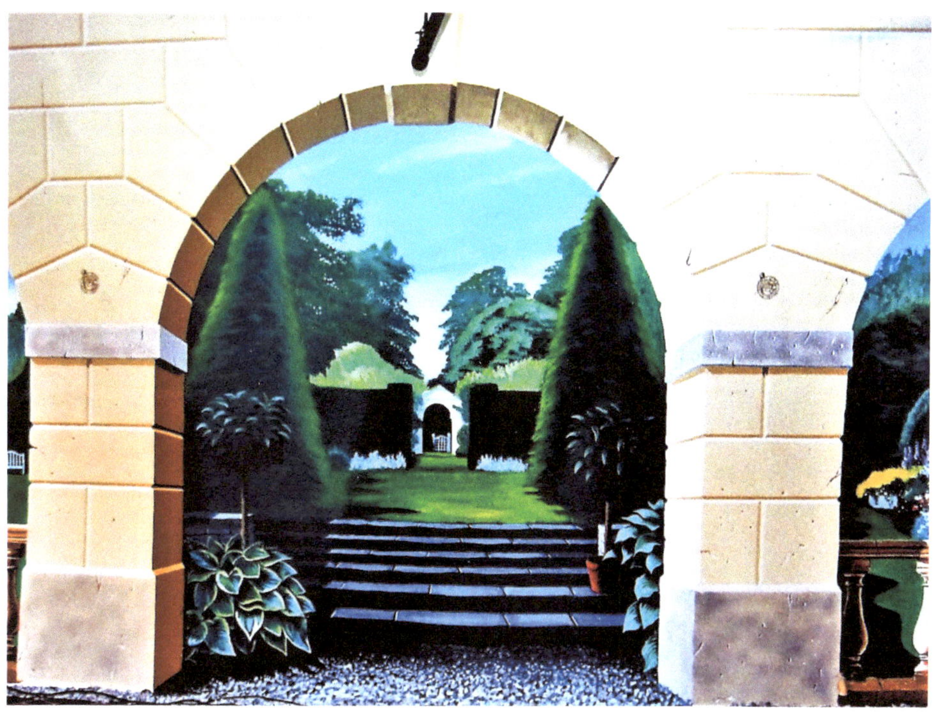

Above and below: Palm Beach Roof Garden Restaurant, 1990.

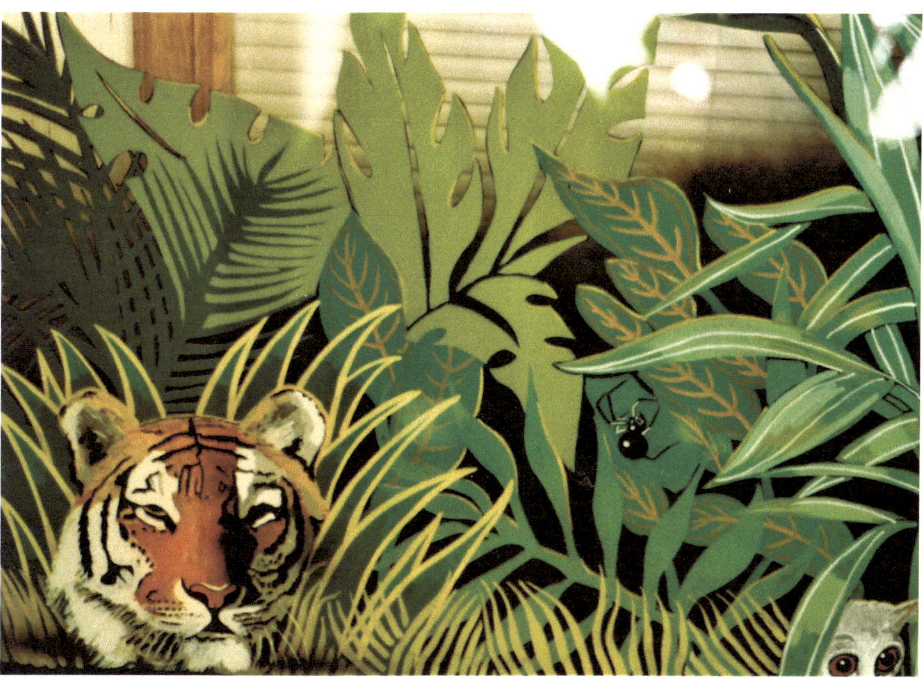

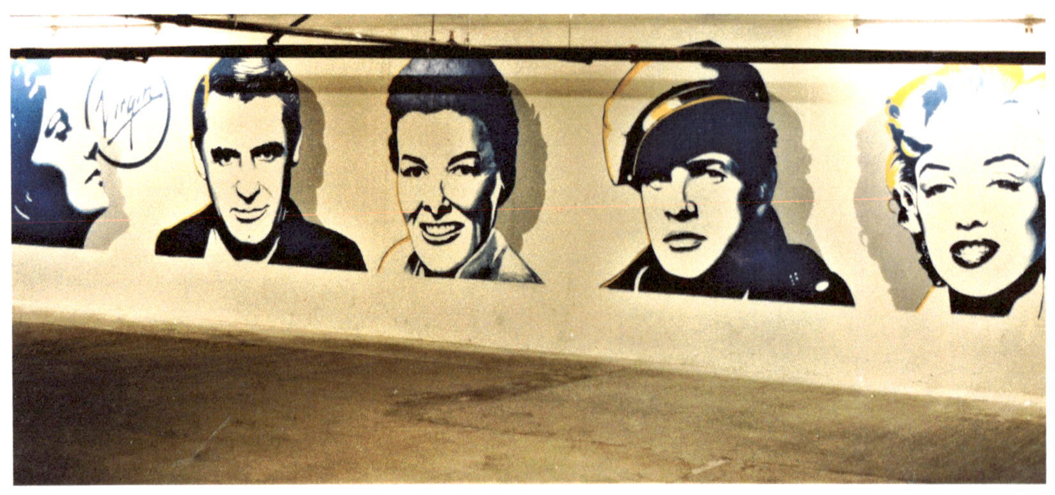

Virgin Megastore car park.

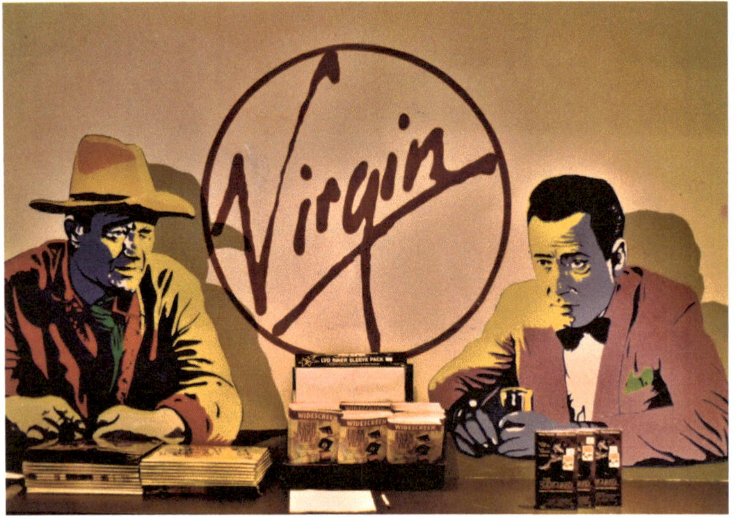

Virgin Megastore,
Orange County, 1994.

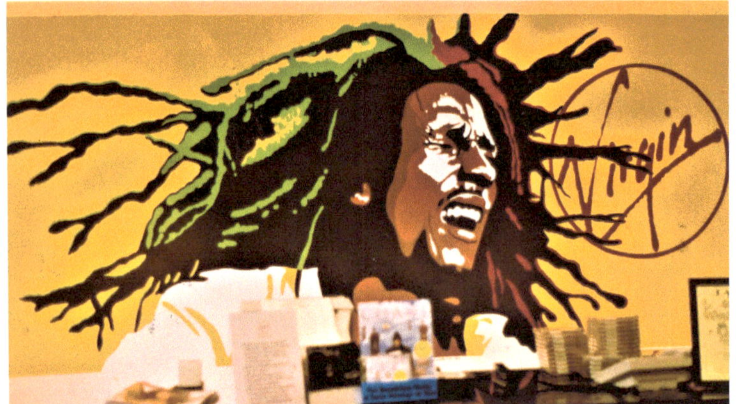

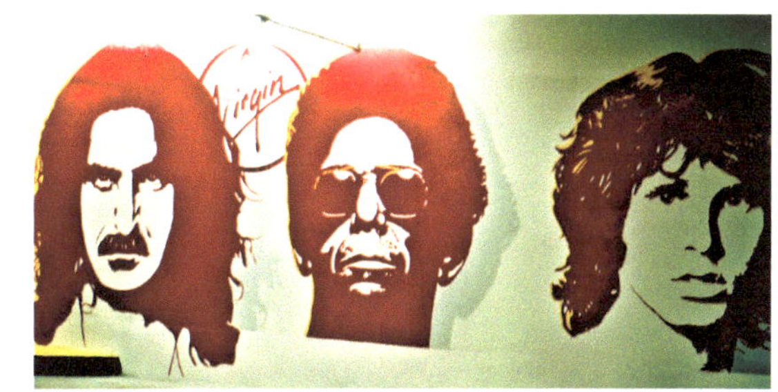

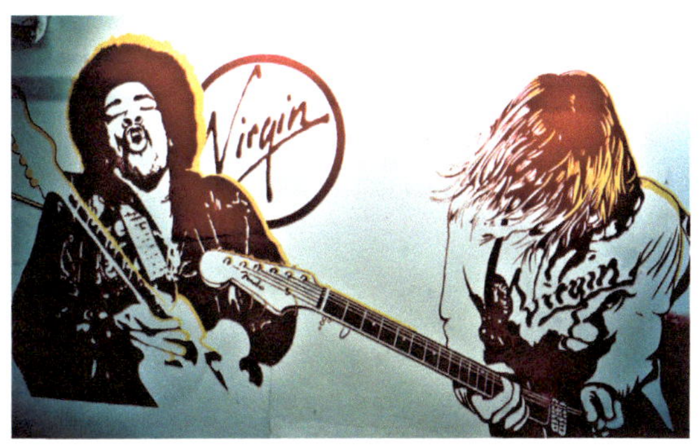

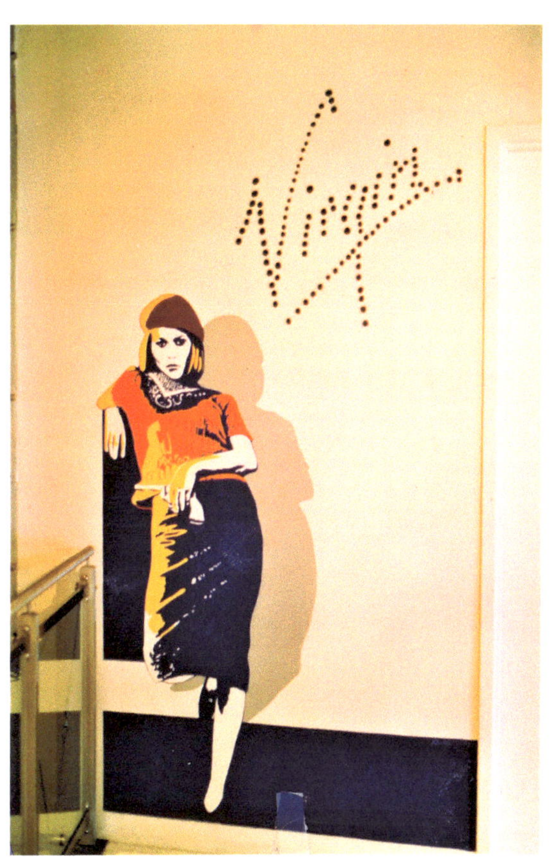

Virgin Megastore, Los Angeles, 1994.

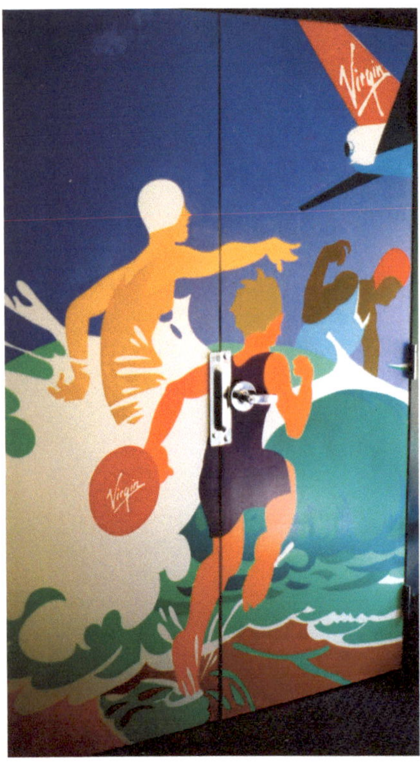

Virgin Atlantic Offices, Connecticut, 1995.

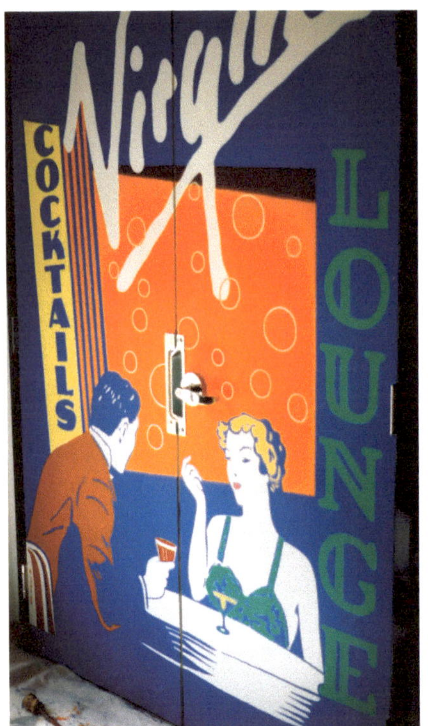

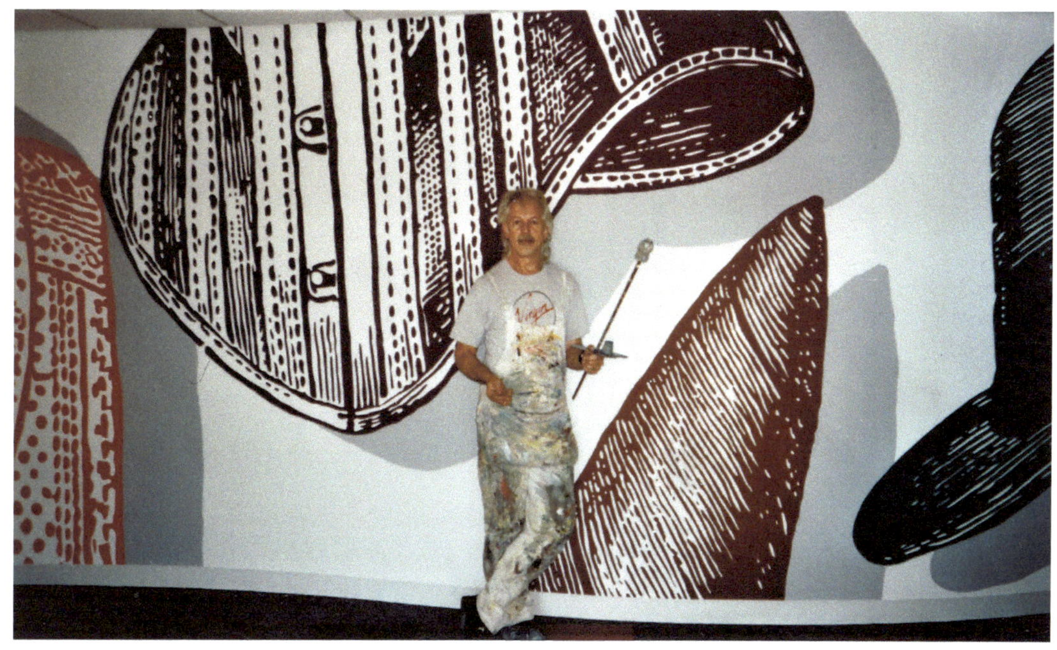

Ken at work at the Virgin Atlantic Offices, Connecticut, in 1997.

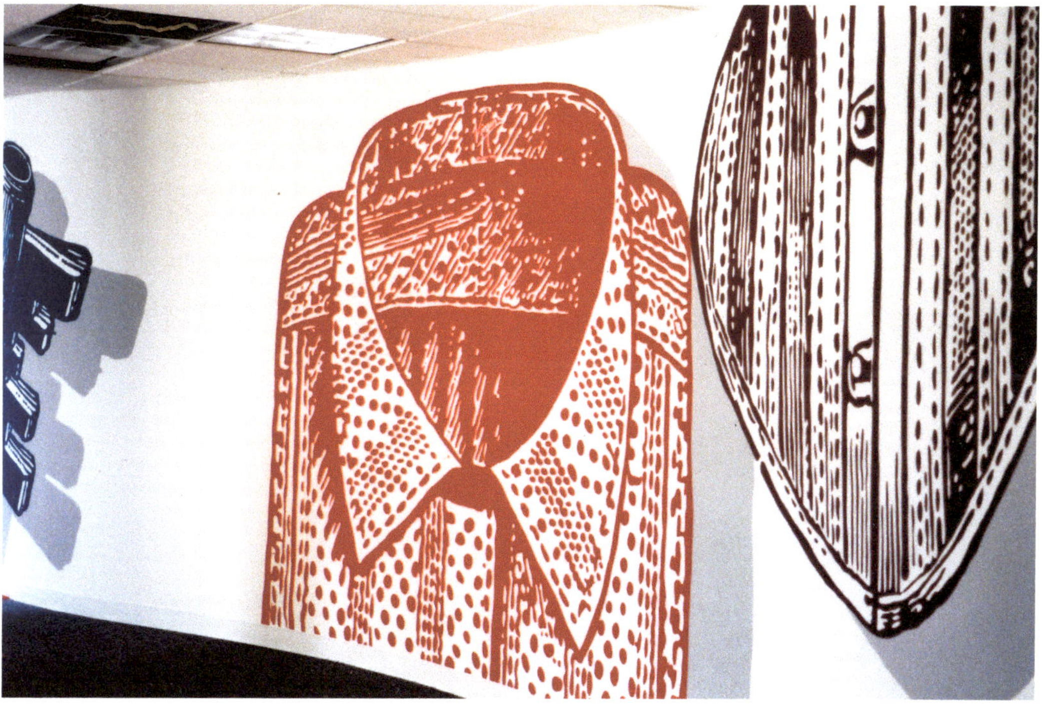

Virgin Atlantic Offices, Connecticut 4: 1997

The End of an Era

By 2004 the Virgin empire had grown too big for Branson to keep his snazzy knitwear-clad arms around it. The accountants became gatekeepers and the business relationship between Ken and Branson became sustainable no longer.

In the two decades that Ken worked for Virgin he'd neither signed a contract nor had the value of his retainer increased. But he did travel the world at both the company's behest and its first-class expense.

The Scarlet Lady

Murals, as discussed, are transient things. Hence, as with the Swindon murals, it's likely that the Virgin murals are also now all gone. Yet there is one enduring symbol of Ken's period with Virgin.

When in the early stages of planning his airline's corporate identity, Branson expressed a desire for a logo people would recognise at once, and it had to be something that broke with the staid conventions of the day. The notion of nose-cone art, similar to that painted on Second World War fighters and bombers, piqued his interest, so he instructed Ken to produce something along those lines.

The resulting image was formed from a hybrid of ideas, including Second World War cone-art and the work of the Peruvian pin-up artist Alberto Vargas – a contributor to *Playboy Magazine* in the latter part of his career.

Ken carried out the design work in his Swindon studio then took five large airbrush drawing ideas to a meeting with Richard and Virgin design and aircraft staff. They decided on the Scarlet Lady to go the Boeing's American works. There, Boeing reproduced it on a 20-foot-long transfer and heat-sealed it onto an aircraft's fuselage.

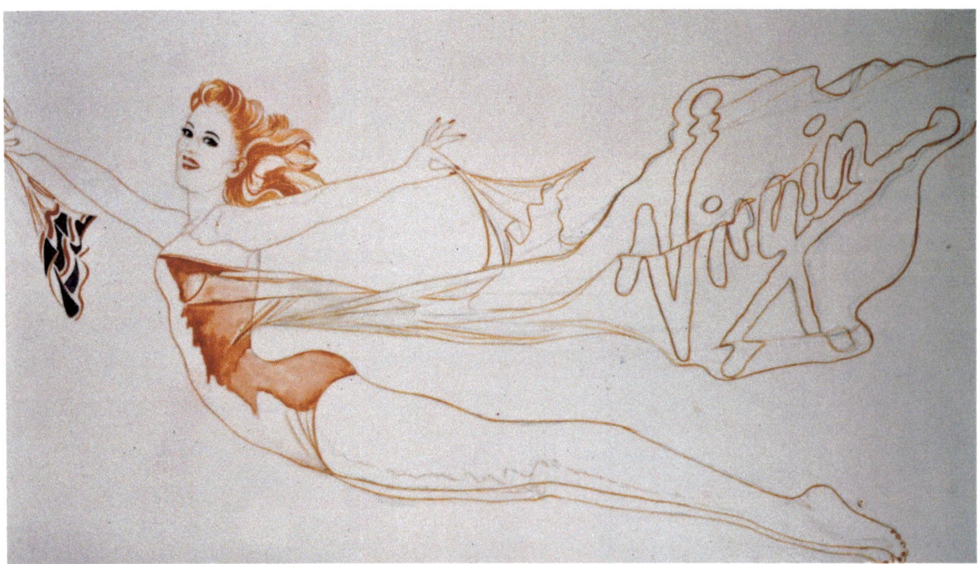

Above and opposite page: The Scarlet Lady, 1986.

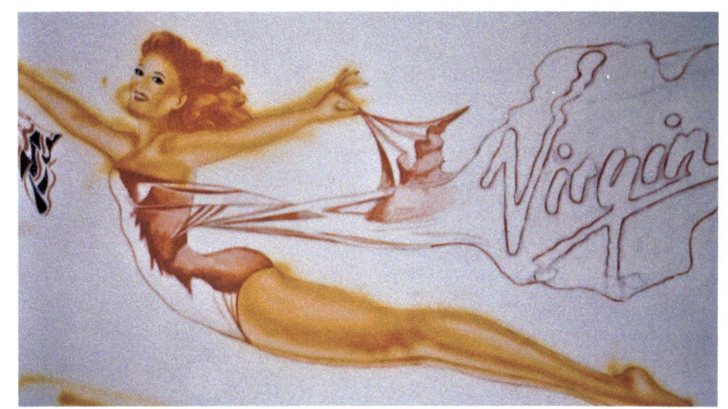

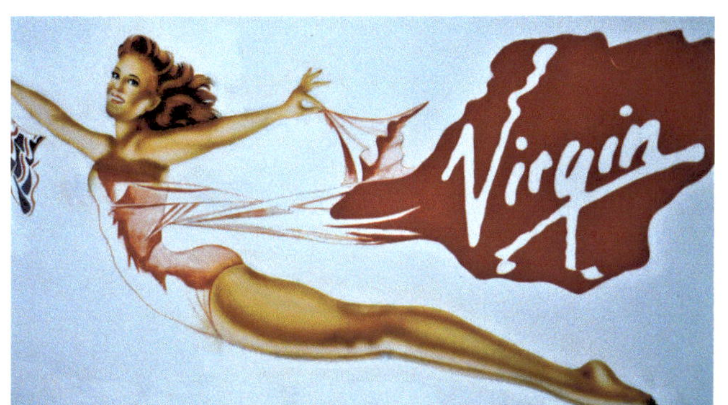

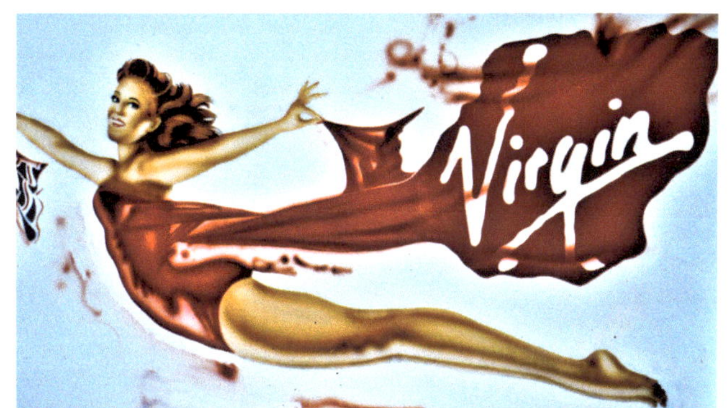

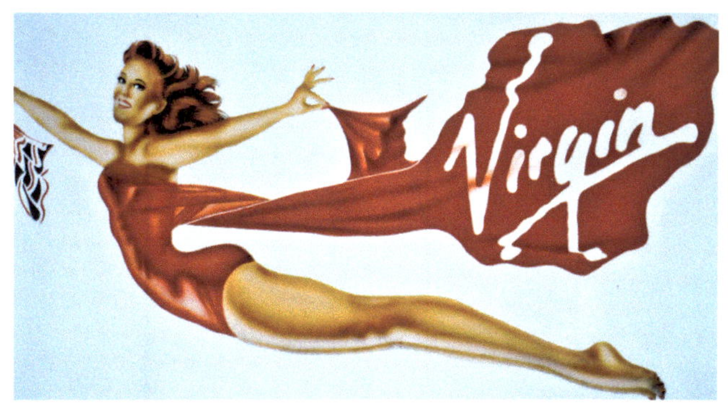

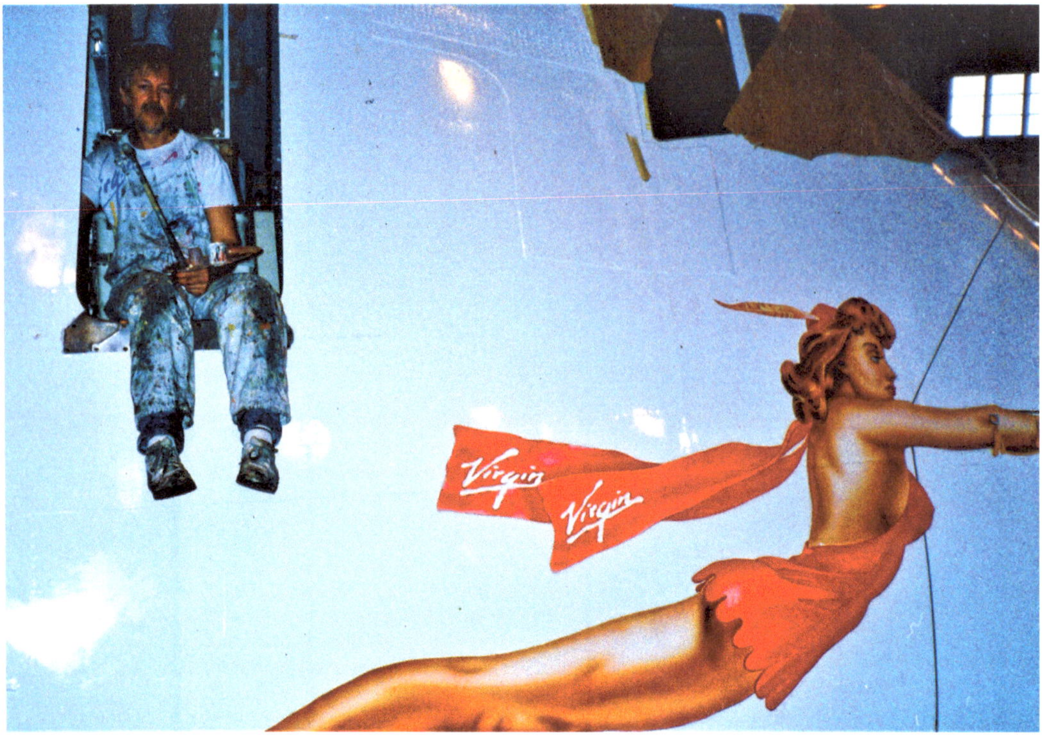

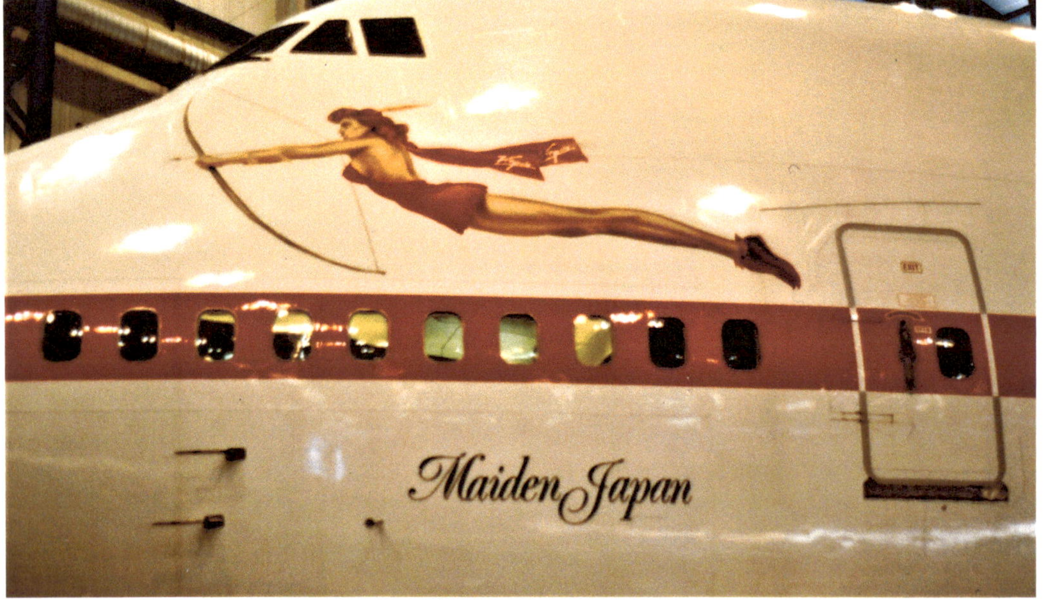

Maiden Japan 747 showing Ken at work in 1989.

Maiden Japan 747, 1989.

Chapter 5

Everybody's Talking about Pop Music: Music Magazine and Albums

In 1980, home-grown new-wave band XTC released *Black Sea* – their fourth studio album. Ken painted the sky and seascape backdrop for the cover. Then Andy Partridge sketched out the design of a flying seagull, a ship's mast and a waning moon that together spelled out the band's name.

Ken also designed for *The Affair*, as well as for performances and concerts at the Wyvern Theatre and the Oasis Leisure dome.

During his art college years, Ken met Raymond O'Sullivan – the son of an Irish family that had moved to Swindon. Ray went on to adopt Gilbert as a stage name and became a popular and successful singer-songwriter. The pair remain friends. Here too Ken met one Richard Davies – born on Eastcott Hill. Better known by the short-form Rick, he went on to become the keyboard-bashing founder of the rock band Supertramp.

Well before *Breakfast in America* became a big hit, Ken, Raymond O'Sullivan and five other art students decided that Swindon offered no outlet for their talents. So, in the manner of Dick Whittington, off to London they went. Renting a house in Notting Hill (pre-Richard Curtis and gentrification) they put Swindon on the nameplate beside the door and went in search of work. Ken kipped under the stairs. In the fullness of time the housemates went their separate ways. For a couple of years Ray and Ken shared a one-room flat above a shop selling Catholic literature and artefacts in Needham Road, Westbourne Grove.

The friendship between these three has continued through the years, with Ken's association with Raymond O'Sullivan being particularly strong. In 1974 Ken painted the singer's portrait and designed posters for his shows – in particular his 1978 tour. In 1981, when Ray, his wife Aase, their daughter Helen and their collie dog Leo all lived in Southern Ireland, Ken painted a group picture of them all for the family home.

Come 2004, Ken's enduring association with Ray O'Sullivan surfaced once more when Ken designed the artwork for *Caricature,* the singer's boxed set of albums. The work included a woodcut portrait of the singer with a large 'G' on his chest.

And now for a snippet of pop trivia: on the 1969 track 'Mr Moody's Garden', you can hear Ken as backing vocal. Not a lot of people know that!

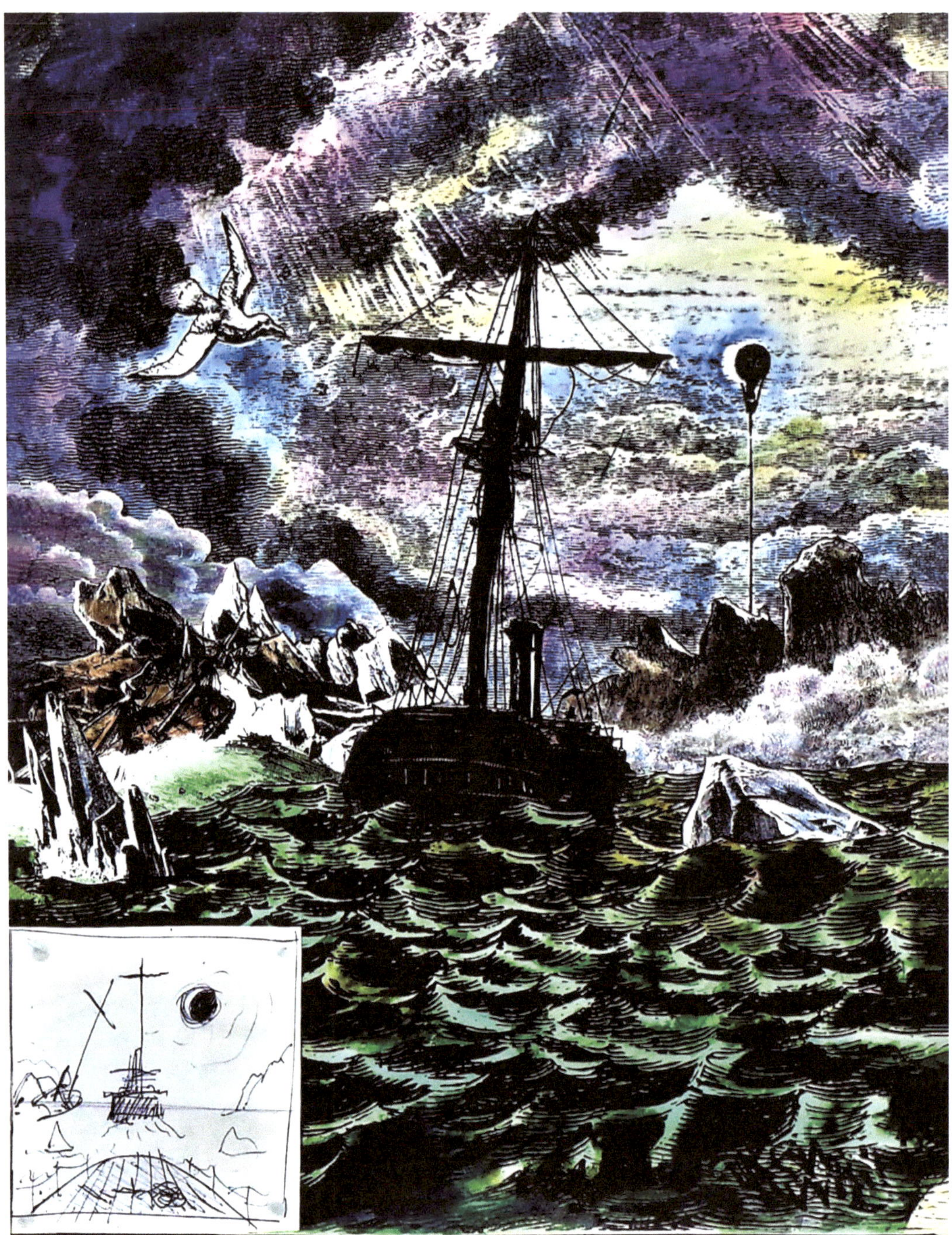

Original drawing for the XTC album cover.

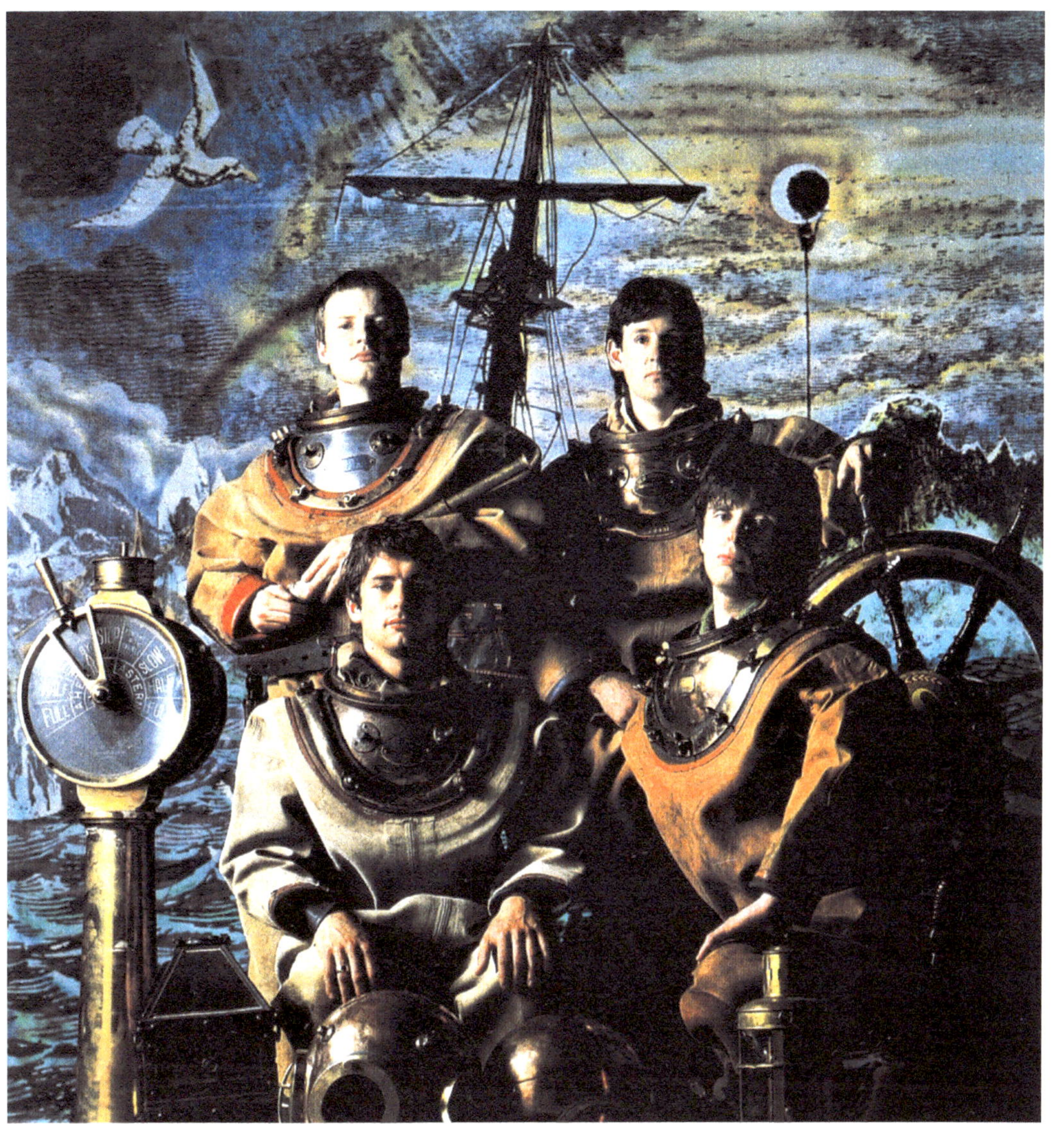

The finished XTC album cover.

As seen already, during the 1960s Ken produced illustrations for teen magazines, for feminist magazines and for cultural comment magazines. In the 1970s his magazine work continued but with pop magazines – notably *Cream Magazine*. This short-lived magazine, published in London W1 by Arapel Ltd, sat on the newsagent's shelves from May 1971 to August 1973. During that time, the magazine featured illustrations or paintings by Ken of Alice Cooper, David Bowie and Ian Anderson, both on the magazine cover and in its pages.

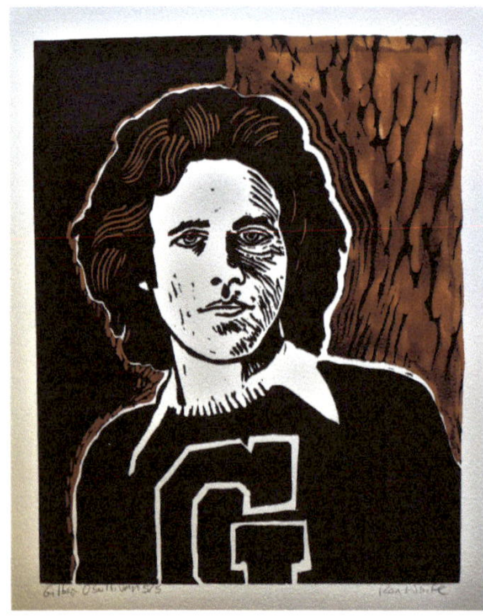

Left: The Gilbert 'G' linocut.

Below: Gilbert O'Sullivan's *Caricature* album cover linocut.

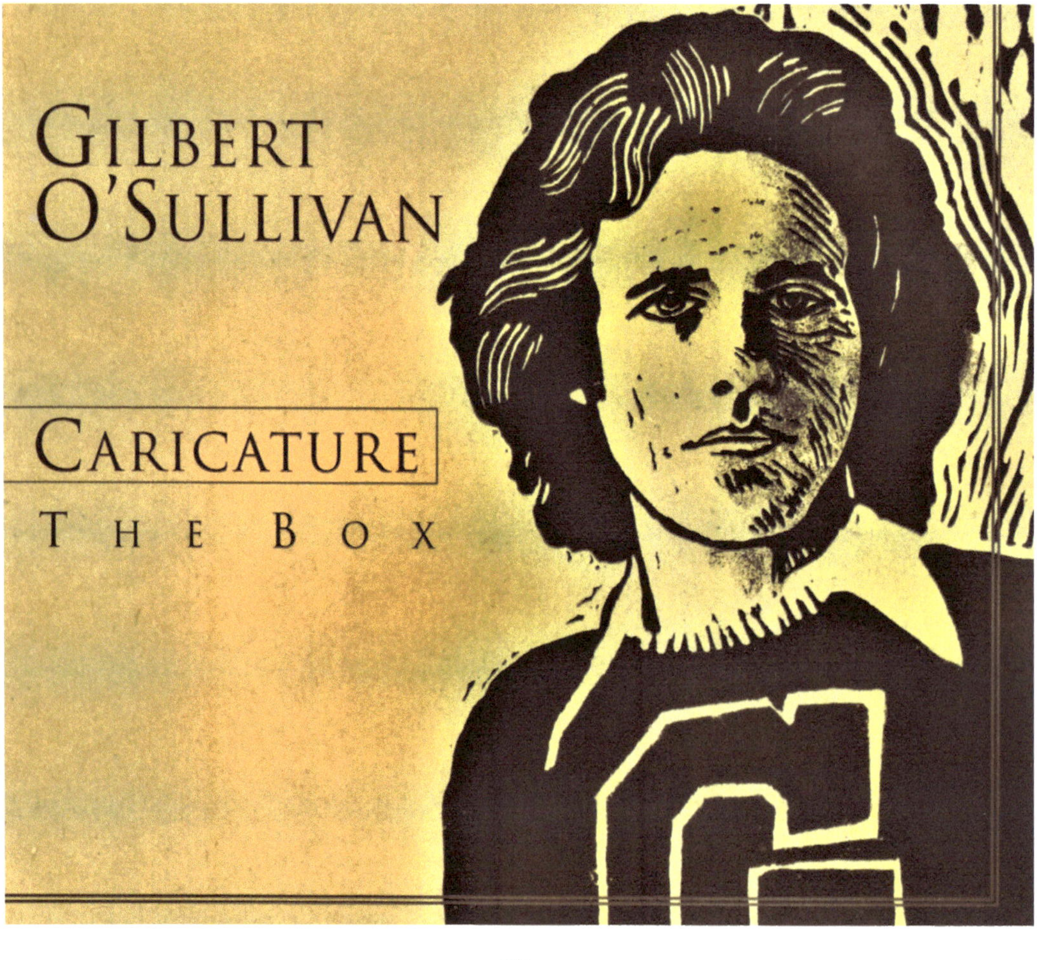

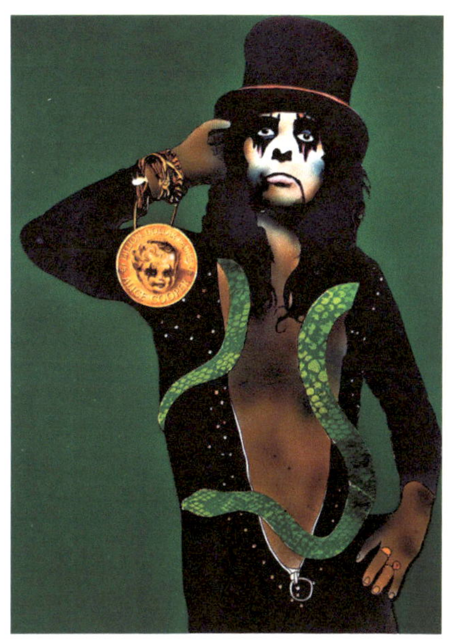

Alice Cooper artwork.

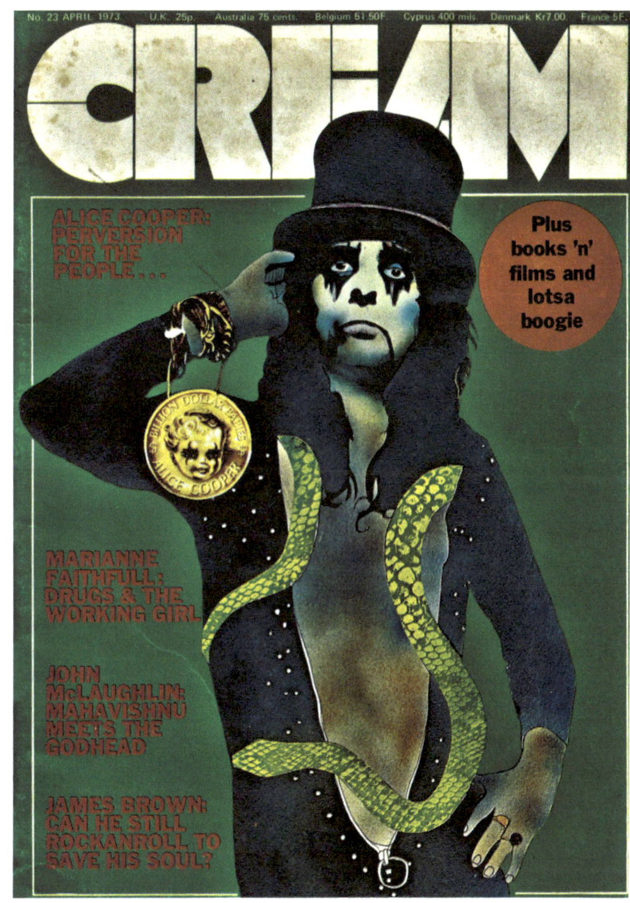

Alice Cooper for the cover of *Cream* magazine.

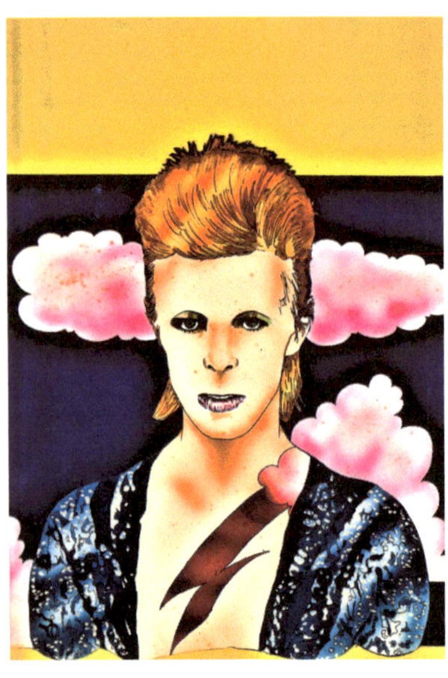

David Bowie original drawing.

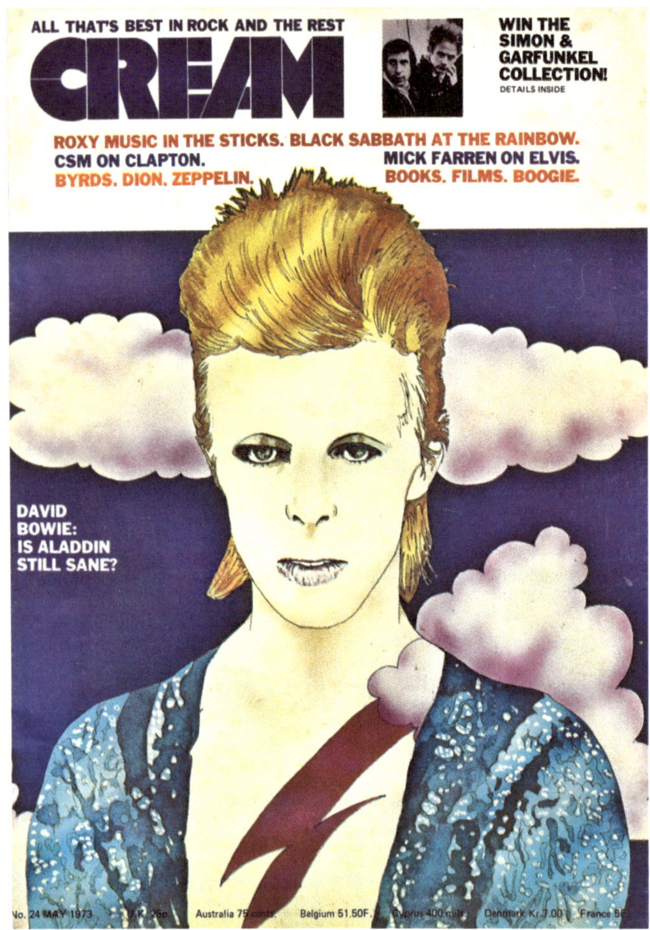

David Bowie for the cover of *Cream* magazine.

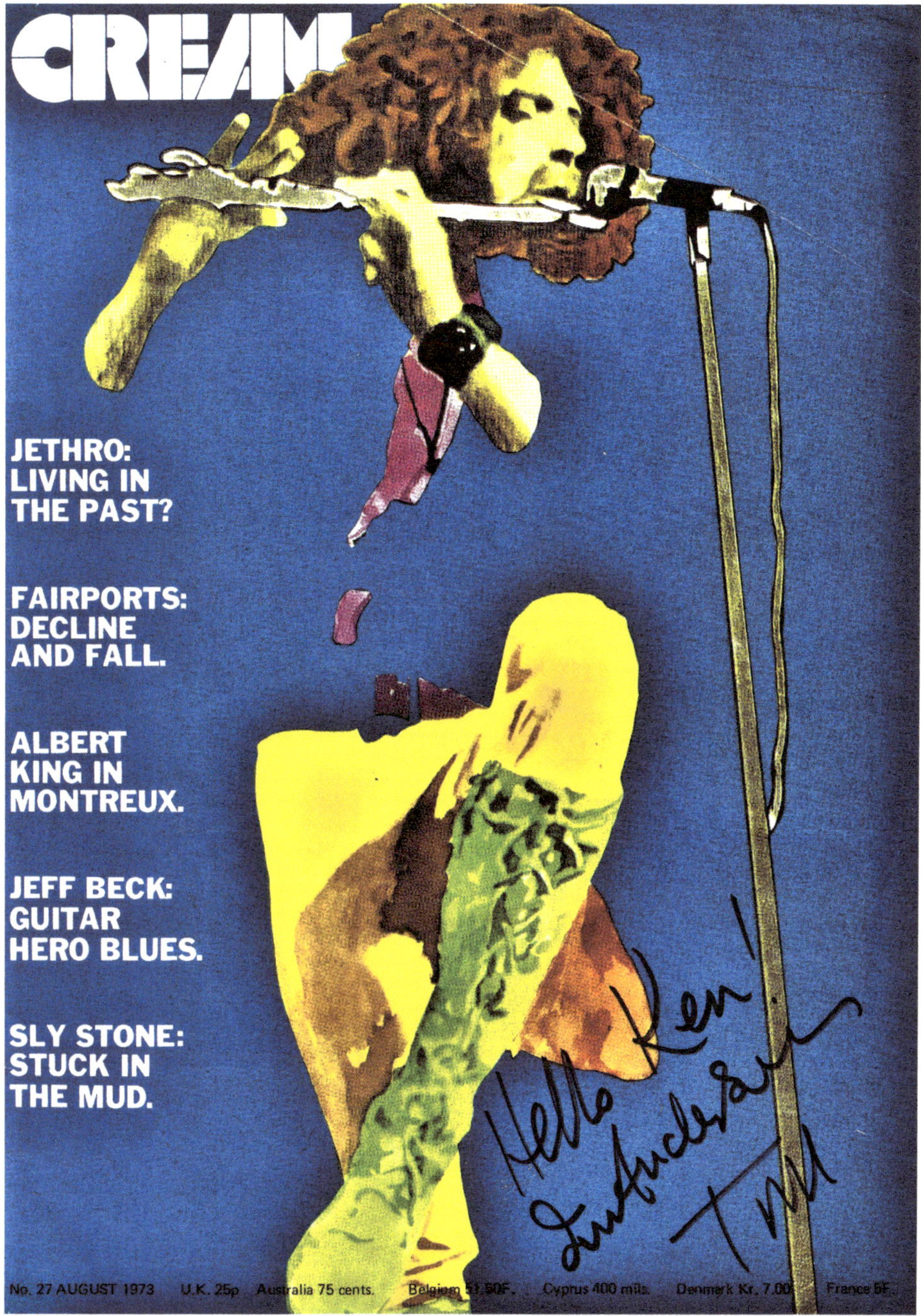

Ian Anderson for the cover of *Cream* magazine.

Chapter 6

Living in the Shadow of the Works: Paintings and Linocuts

A further important strand to Ken's work is as chronicler of particular elements of Swindon's twentieth-century past – chiefly of life in and around the Works. Via his art, Ken narrates his home town's bleak, drab industrial past. He shows the toiling of the labouring classes – those that brought the town to the brink of post-war prosperity, but were too old to then share in its benefits. Ken's later works reflect this version of Swindon.

There couldn't be a sharper contrast between his ongoing industrial chronicles and the joyful anarchy seen in so much of his *Trompe-l'œil* work and his murals. In so many of them the day is super sunny and the sky or its reflections in windows are the brightest, bluest of blues.

A Proper Job

A 'proper job' in Swindon in the 1950s, as indeed with any working-class town, constituted one holding the promise of stability and longevity. No employer had a greater record in that respect or held a better prospect for the future in the Swindon area than British Railways – British Rail from 1965. BR resulted from the 1948 government nationalisation of the rail system that included the former Great Western Railway. By the time nationalisation came around, the GWR had been a huge employer of labour in Swindon for a little over a century. During this time countless sons had followed their fathers into the Works. The White family were no exception.

In this way, three generations of the White family worked inside: Ken's grandfather, father, uncles, and his brother Mike, who started there as a fitter and turner. As mentioned, when the fifteen-year-old Ken left secondary education in 1958 he trod his brother's path into the Works, as an unskilled rivet hotter. Imagine spending all day standing in front of a fire, heating up bits of metal for use in the ear-splitting, hell-hot riveting shop. That constituted Ken's working day. When he entered a working environment little changed from 1915, when Alfred Williams (aka the Hammerman Poet) published his experiences in his *Life in a Railway Factory*.

Etched into the psyche of Alfred Williams and into Ken and into everyone who walked through the doors to the sound of the infamous and ubiquitous GWR hooter, is the blood, sweat and toil of the railway workshops. The thud, thud, thud of the steam hammer, the hot rods and the anvils, and the fiery furnaces are built both into Swindon's DNA and the style and the subject of a great deal of Ken's artistic output. In these works, one can almost feel the white-hot heat, the sparks searing the skin. The urge to duck to avoid flying shards of molten metal almost overwhelms.

In Ken's smaller images are sombre and grim-seeming moments of railway workers' lives. As with a snapshot, the paint on the canvas imprisons forever the hard, dull, repetitive, mind-numbing nature of their work. This is a Swindon that no longer exists in the physical sense, yet about which there are strong memories and a fierce pride. Hard and dangerous as this work was, the men and women who toiled in the Works were justly proud of the locomotives they created there. This is the spirit of Swindon.

In the 1980s the Works closed for good, and from the ashes of the old industry rose, phoenix like, a new one: shopping. BAA McArthur Glen converted much of the GWR works into an outlet shopping centre – one of the most successful Outlet Villages in the country in fact. McArthur Glen's CE, Joe Kaempfer, took seven of Ken's larger industrial scene canvasses. In 1997 three of them went on display in the newly built shopping mall, while the rest hung in his office. A reminder of the old in among the new.

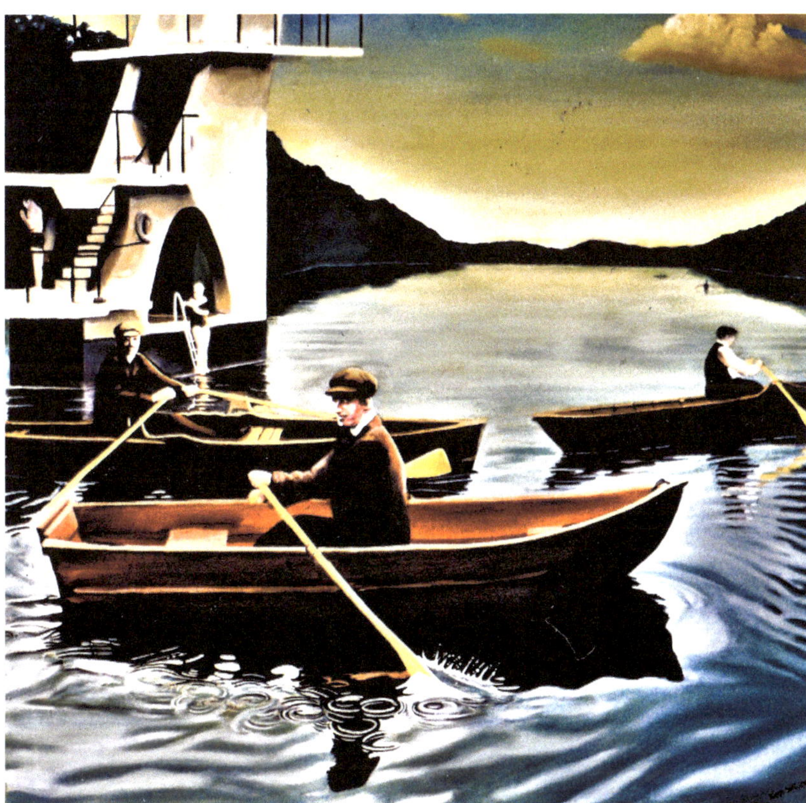

Coate Water.

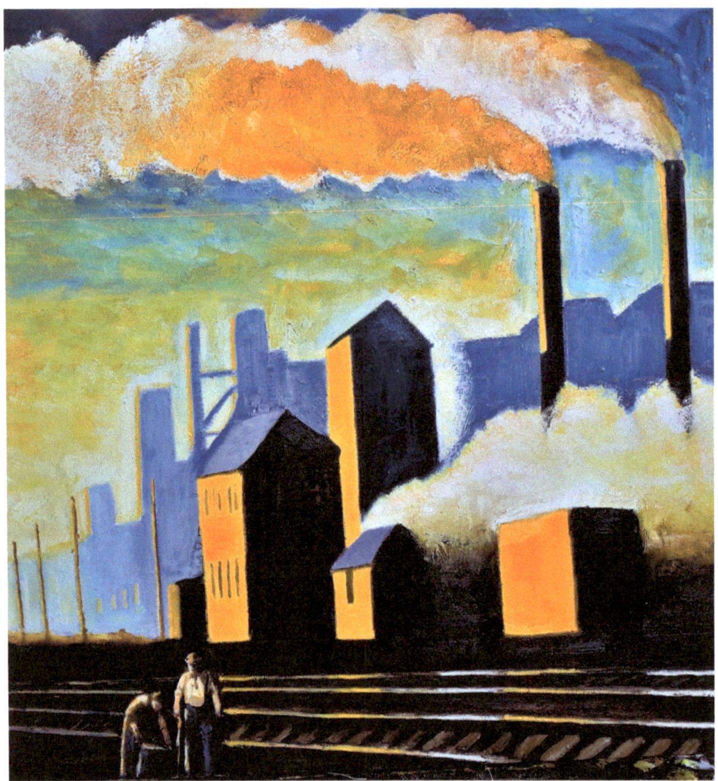

The Gasworks.

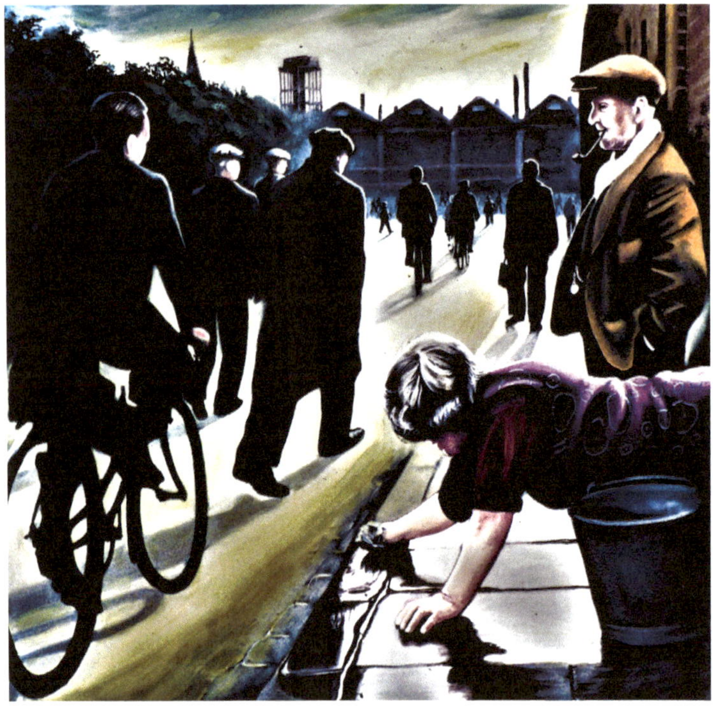

Going to Work.

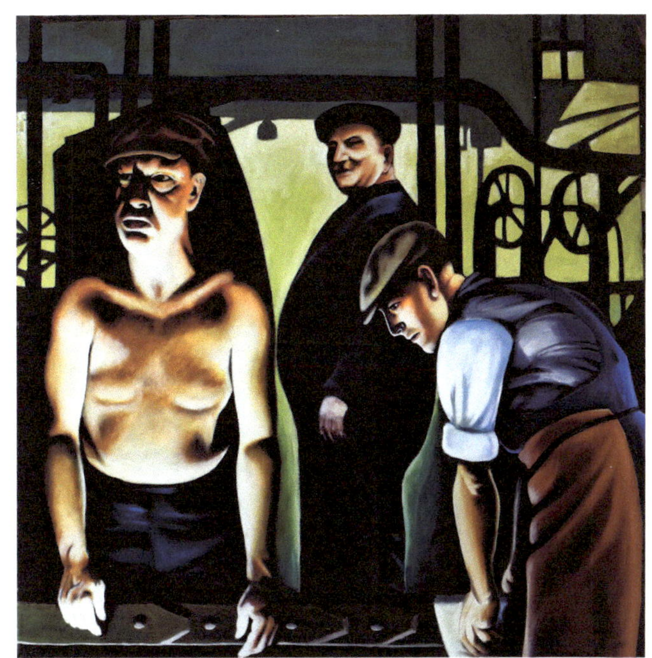

Right: GWR Workers.

Below: Home in the Cold.

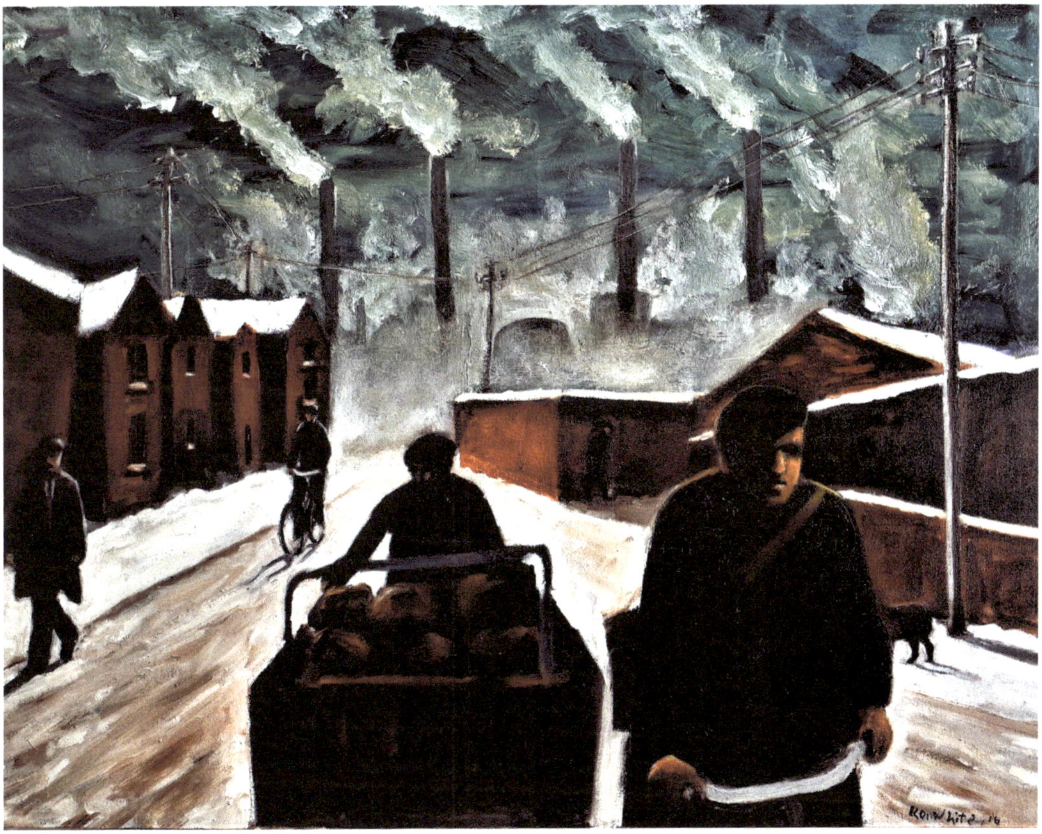

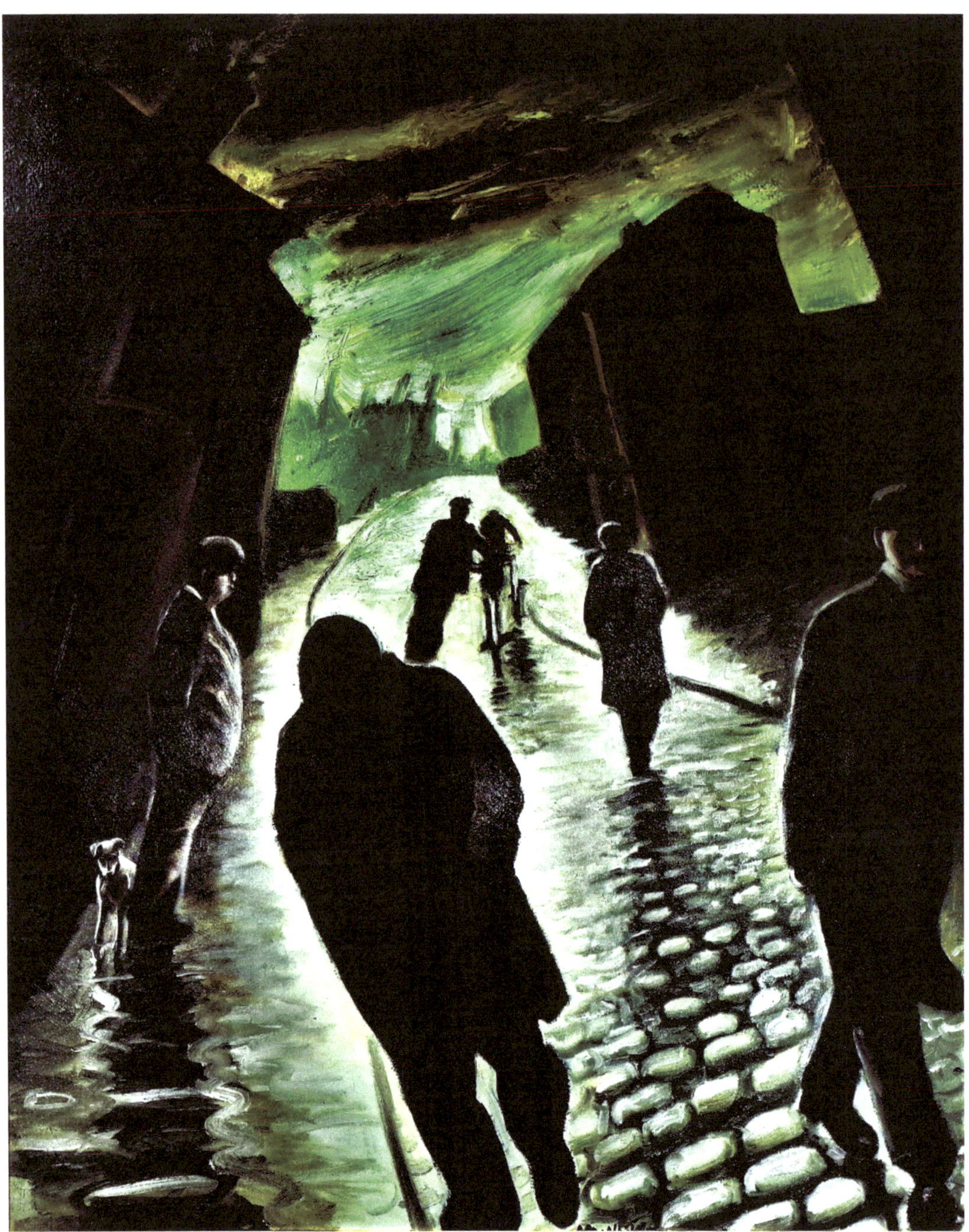

Home in the Wet.

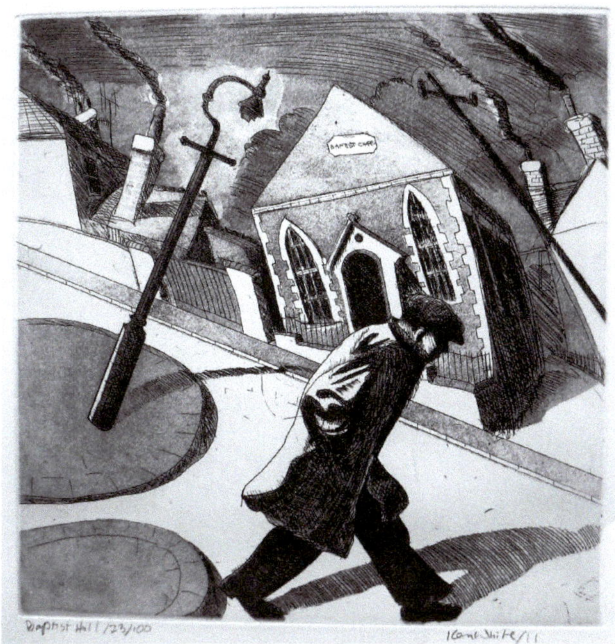

Right: *Home Time* – etching.

Below: *In the Snow.*

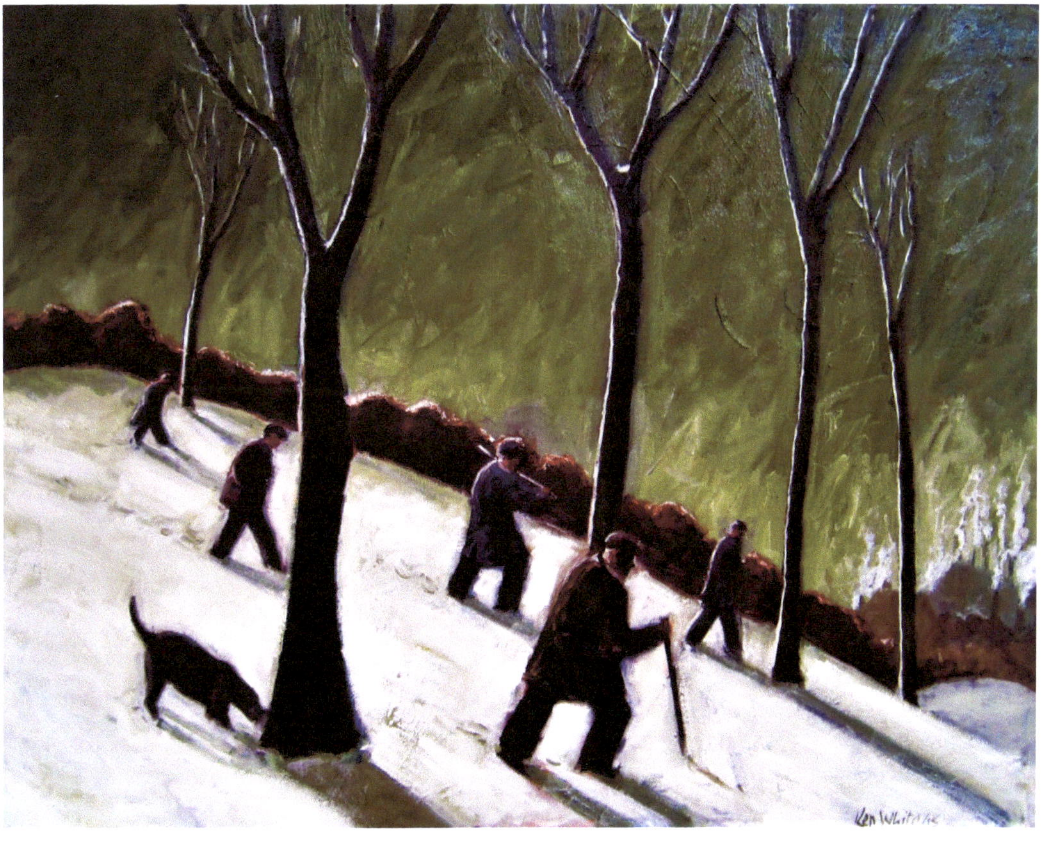

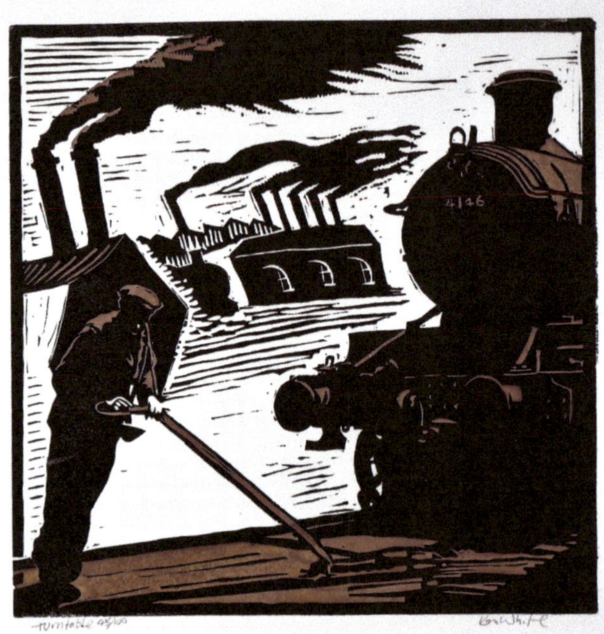

Left, below and opposite page:
Some of Ken's linocuts.

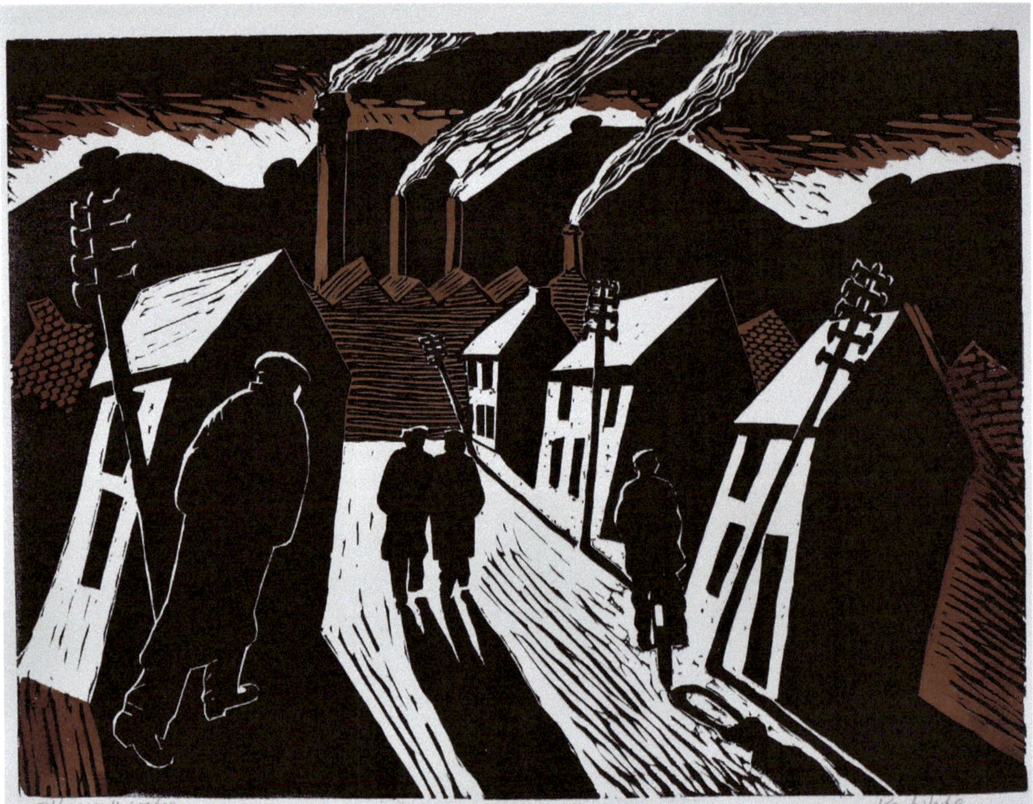

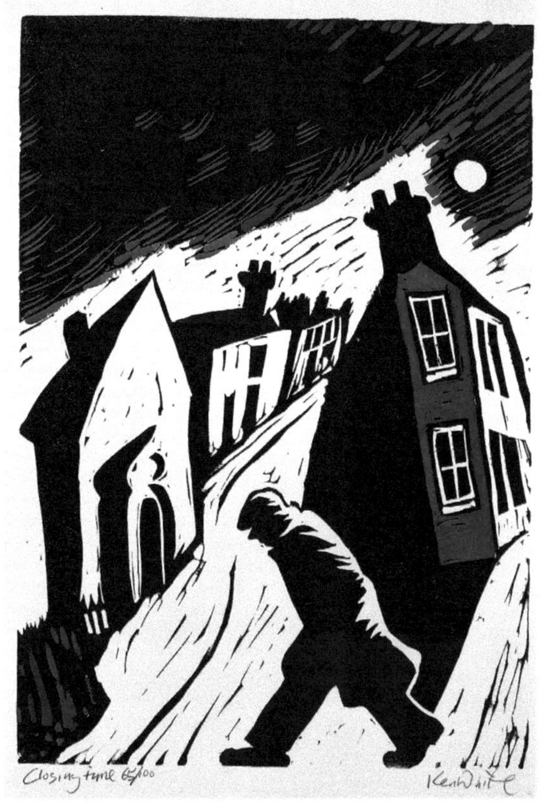

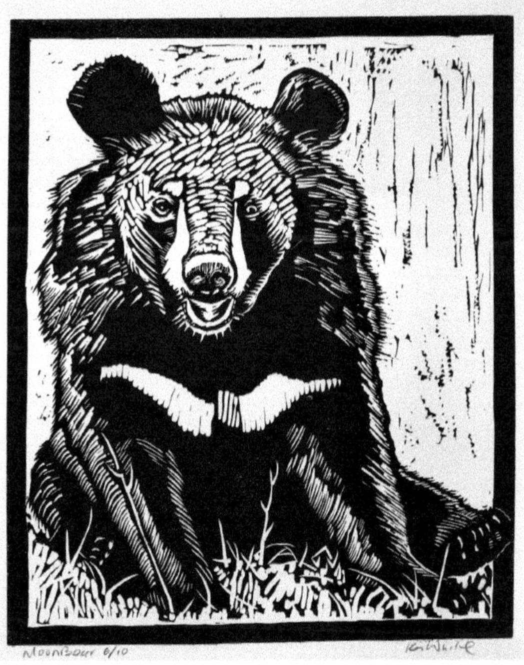

Moon Bear.

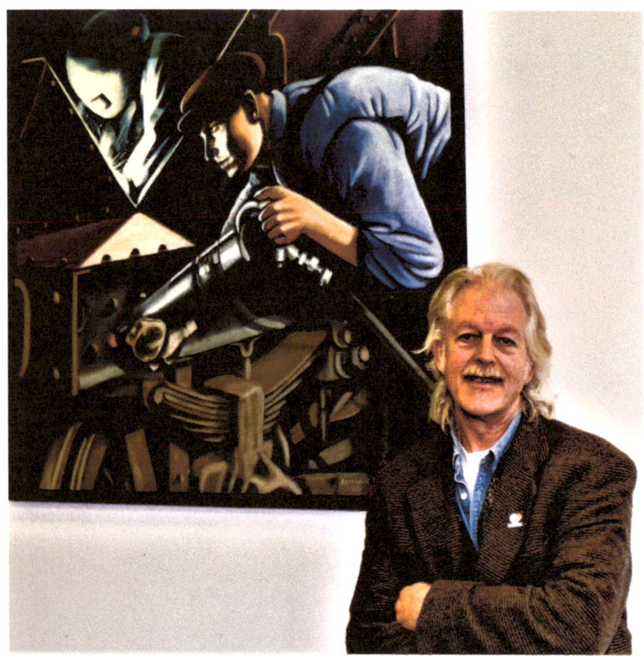

Left: Ken with his riveter painting.

Below: Men in yellow and brown.

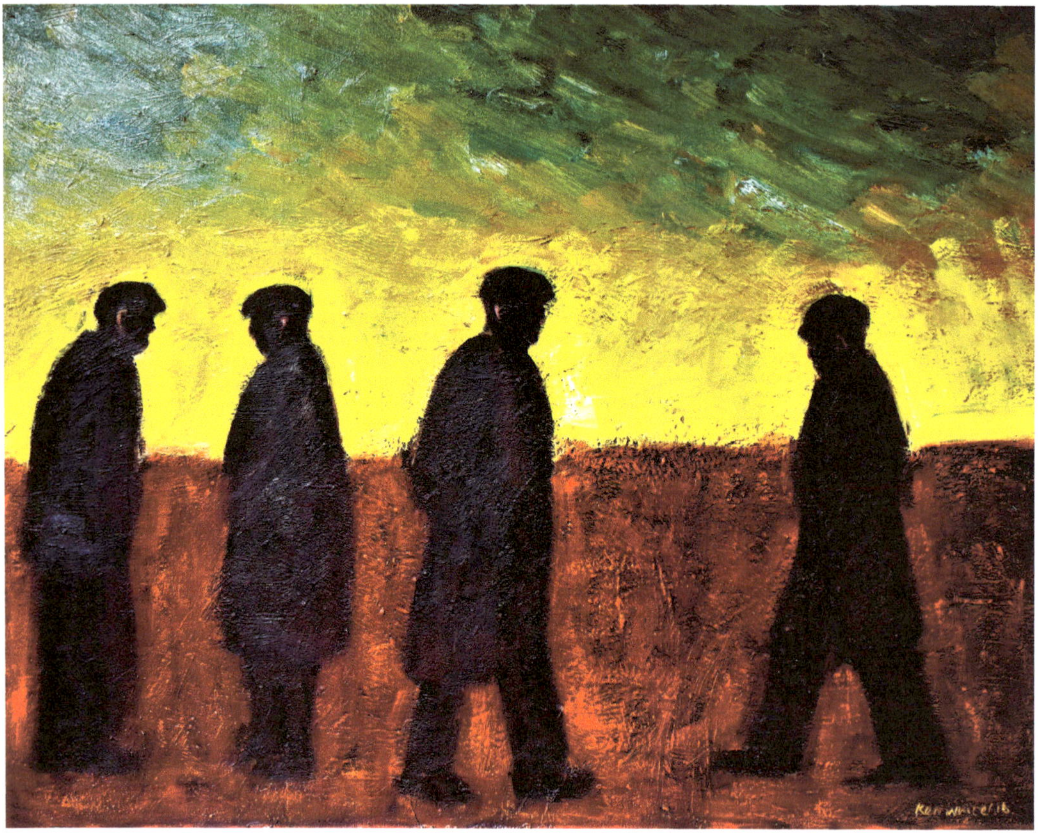

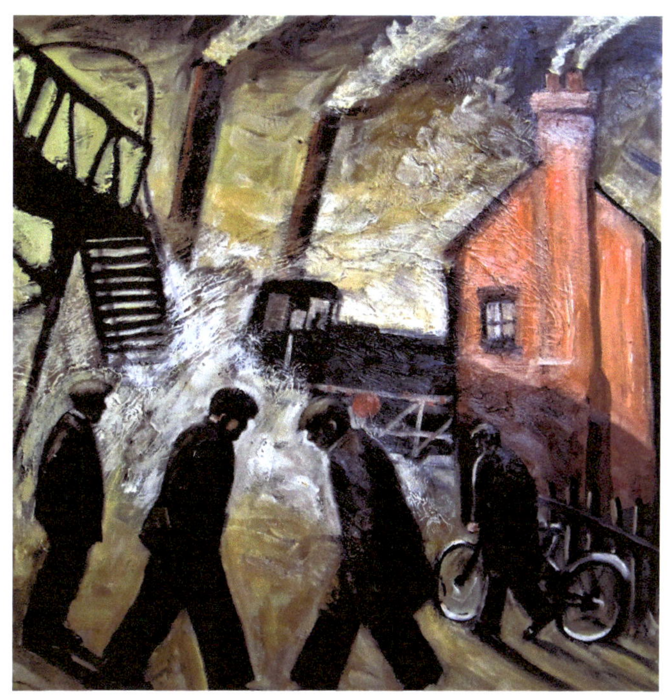

Right: Morning.

Below: Ploughing.

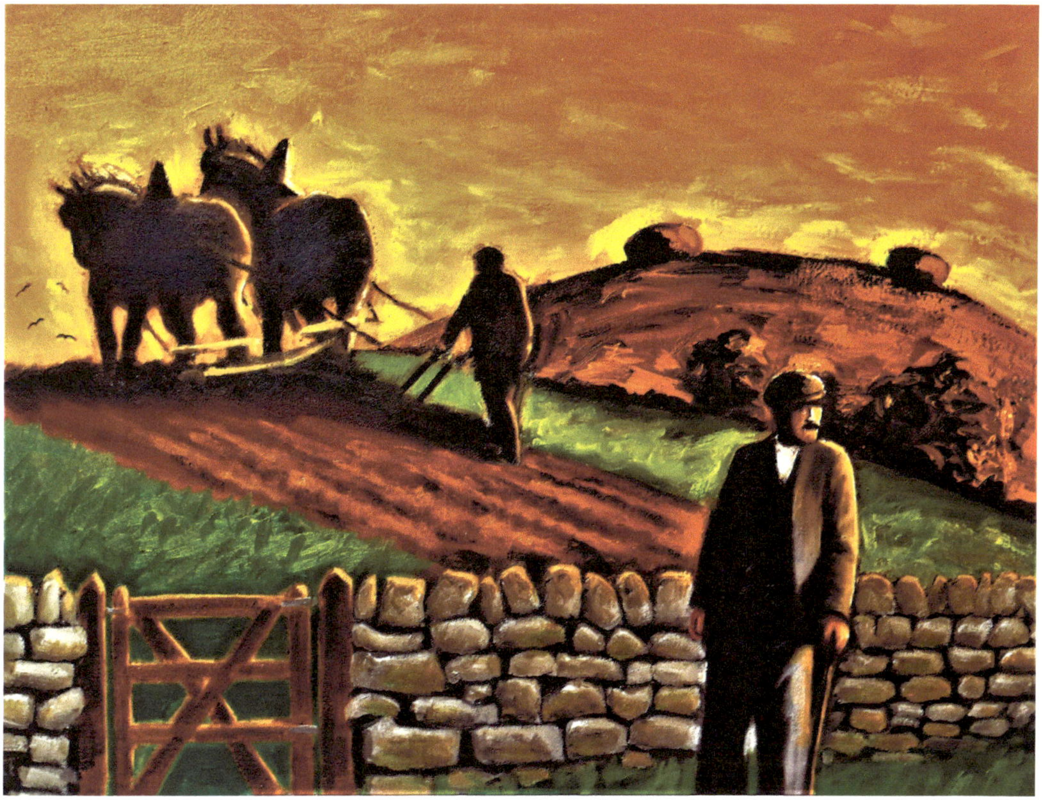

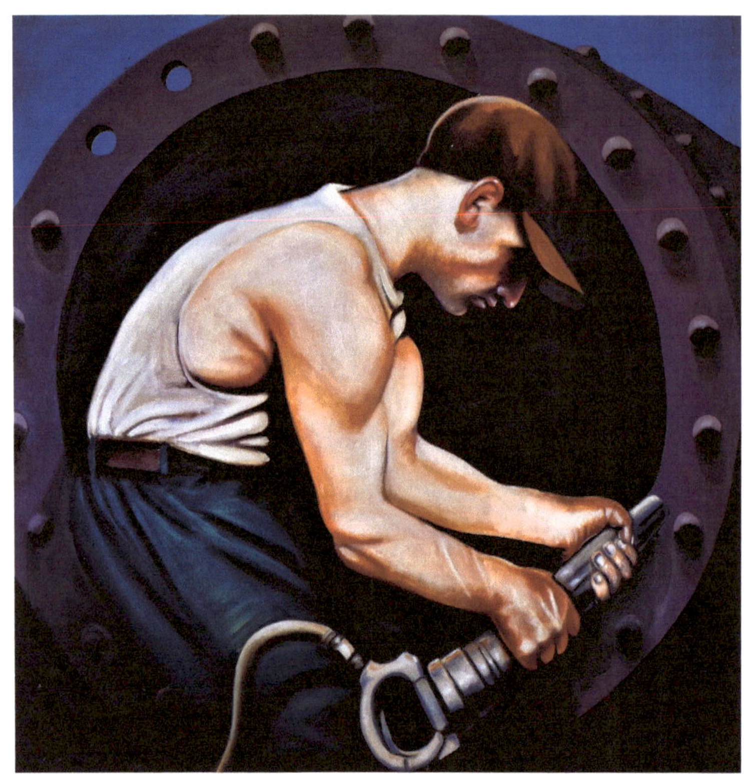

Riveter.

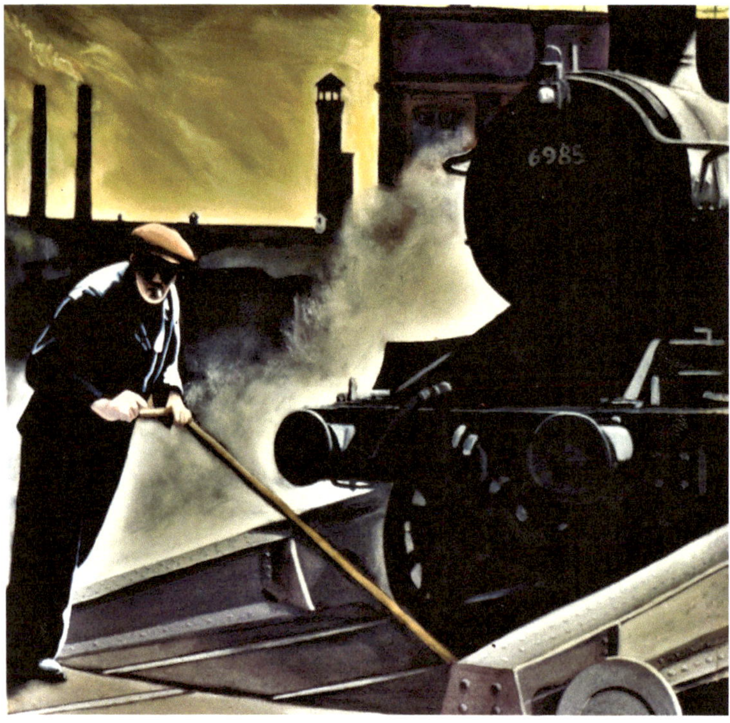

The Locomotive
Turntable.

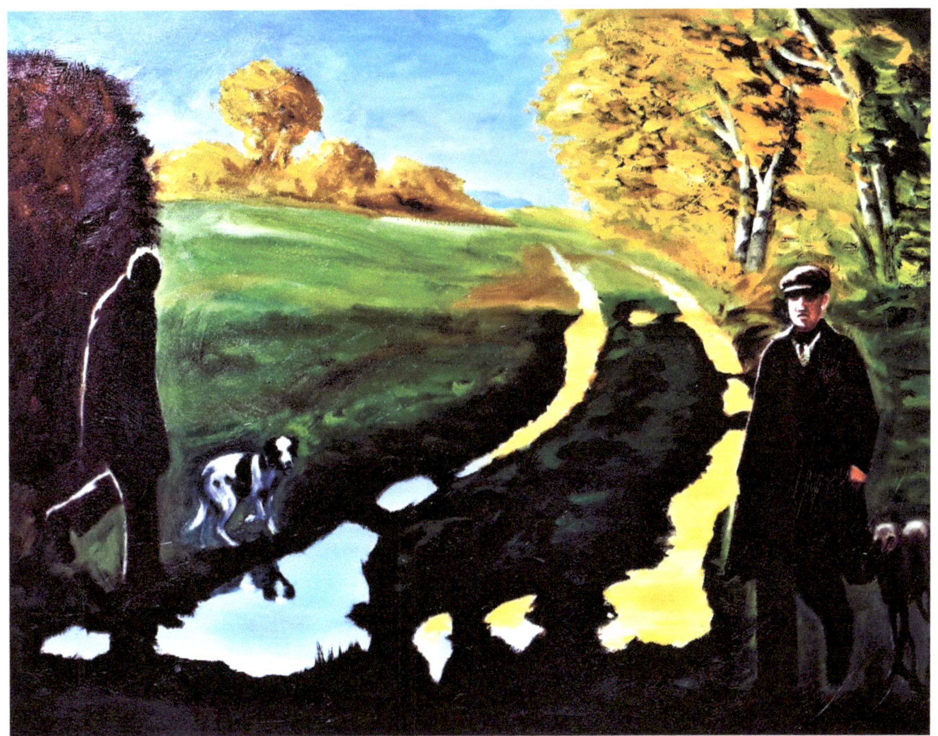

Walking the Dogs.

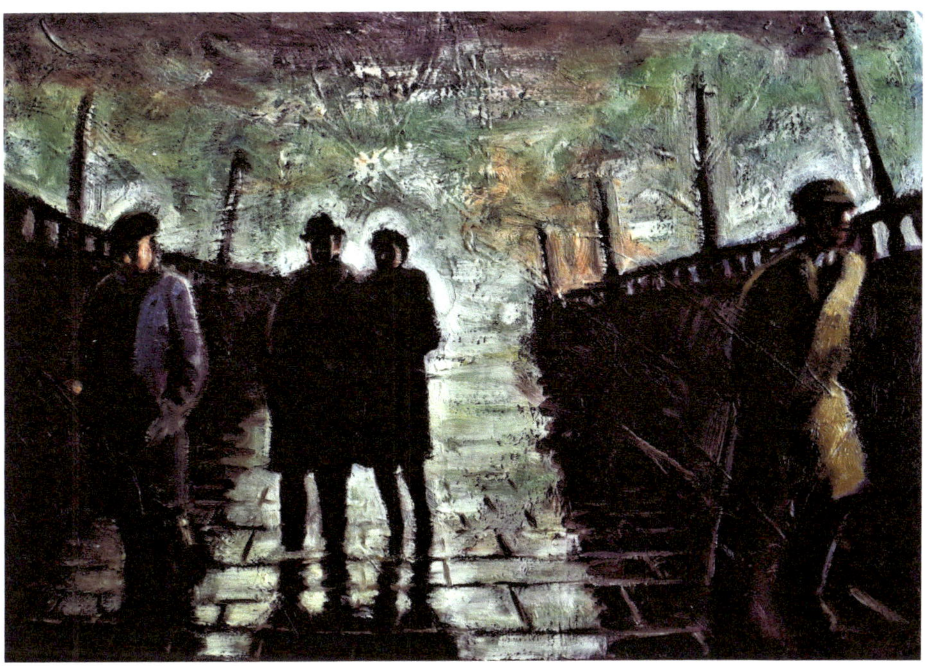

Wet Evening.

Chapter 7

Ken's Work on Show

Murals are, by their nature, impermanent. It's inevitable that we lose them. Though sad, perhaps that's as it should be. They're commissioned at a particular time, often to reflect that period, and so function as social comment. It's rare that anyone commissions an outdoor mural simply because they can. Murals tend to fulfil a need – such as masking something unpleasant or enhancing something dull and plain. But the elements, changing tastes and demolition programmes do away with most of them in the fullness of time.

Were mural works painted on canvas, their value would increase as they passed between collectors. So thank goodness for photography and the written word and books such as this to record them. References exist to Ken's work in several books on the topic of contemporary murals, some of them illustrated. Additionally, Swindon's local studies section of its central library has an excellent online Flickr photographic collection where one can see most, if not all, of Ken's Swindon murals. And there's his own website too.

Despite his obvious and long-standing connections with London, it was 2008 before Ken exhibited any canvases there. In that year a painting of one of Swindon's oldest Baptist chapels, entitled *Baptist Hill,* went on display at the Royal Academy and at the 2008 Bath Society of Arts exhibition. Knowing a good thing when he saw it, TV presenter and antiques expert Paul Martin, of *Flog It!,* bought it.

The painting went on show again in 2009, this time for an exhibition staged at Swindon's Arts Centre. This exhibition featured works depicting aspects of Swindon and her people in the years between the early 1940s and the early 1960s.

Yet another work, a portrait of Swindon's Havelock Street *c.* 1950, exhibited in an EAC (Elderly Accommodation Council) Art Awards Exhibition, took a prize. A subsequent showing at London's Mall galleries followed.

In 2011, Matthew Hall and Tiffany Panter of London's Panter & Hall gallery chanced to see Ken's work in Devizes. The upshot? Later that same year was Ken's first London exhibition, showing twenty oil-on-canvas pieces. In 2012 the gallery mounted a second Ken White exhibition, showing forty canvases under the title 'Grafters'.

Come 2013 Swindon's Artiste collective staged the first local exhibition of Ken's work, presenting the Virgin Scarlet Lady on the floor of the Post Modern.

2015 saw Ken's work go Stateside when five of his works crossed the Atlantic for display at a New York gallery. His works, including *Bronx Afternoon, Dog Walker* and *The Promised Land,* took the Aschan School as their inspiration. This twentieth-century

US artistic movement is best known for portraying scenes of daily life in the poorer neighbourhoods of New York.

Ken received the *Wiltshire Life Magazine* award for arts and music in 2010. By this time he'd painted over 100 murals worldwide – there's a full list of them in the appendix – with ten or so of them in Swindon.

Swindon has in its possession a fine collection of twentieth-century art – one that bears the reputation of being the finest outside of London's Tate Modern. Up until 2016, this art collection contained nothing of Ken's work. If that seems a lamentable lack of official recognition by the town, his work was and still is appreciated by the townsfolk. Ken has legions of fans among Swindonians, who hold his murals in great affection for their depictions of characters well-known to them from Swindon's industrial, social and cultural history. Likewise, his portraits of life in and around the Works are loved too for their mirroring of lives lived and remembered by many.

However, recent years have brought fresh activity to Swindon's Museum and Art gallery. The curator gives excellent regular, free, lunchtime talks and there's a frequent change of exhibitions. Further, late in 2018, in a first for the museum and art gallery, they asked local artists to submit works for an exhibition in the art gallery.

Before all that though, in 2016, Swindon Borough Council and the Creative Wiltshire project acquired a selection of Ken's works reflecting different aspects of his career. They chose two large atmospheric and active paintings depicting life as a rivet hotter in the GWR Works, along with a print of singer-songwriter Gilbert O'Sullivan. And, to record for posterity something of his mural-painting achievements, Swindon's art collection now boasts Ken's original sketch for the landmark, life-changing Golden Lion mural. What's more, September 2019 sees a Ken White exhibition at Swindon's museum and art gallery.

Thus, as is fitting, Ken's value to Swindon as a chronicler of first-hand experience of life in the town's great GWR Works achieves appreciation and endorsement by the town of his birth.

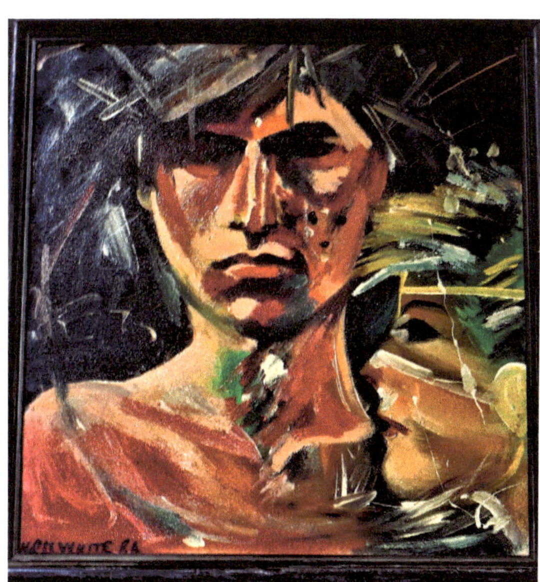

The 1980s.

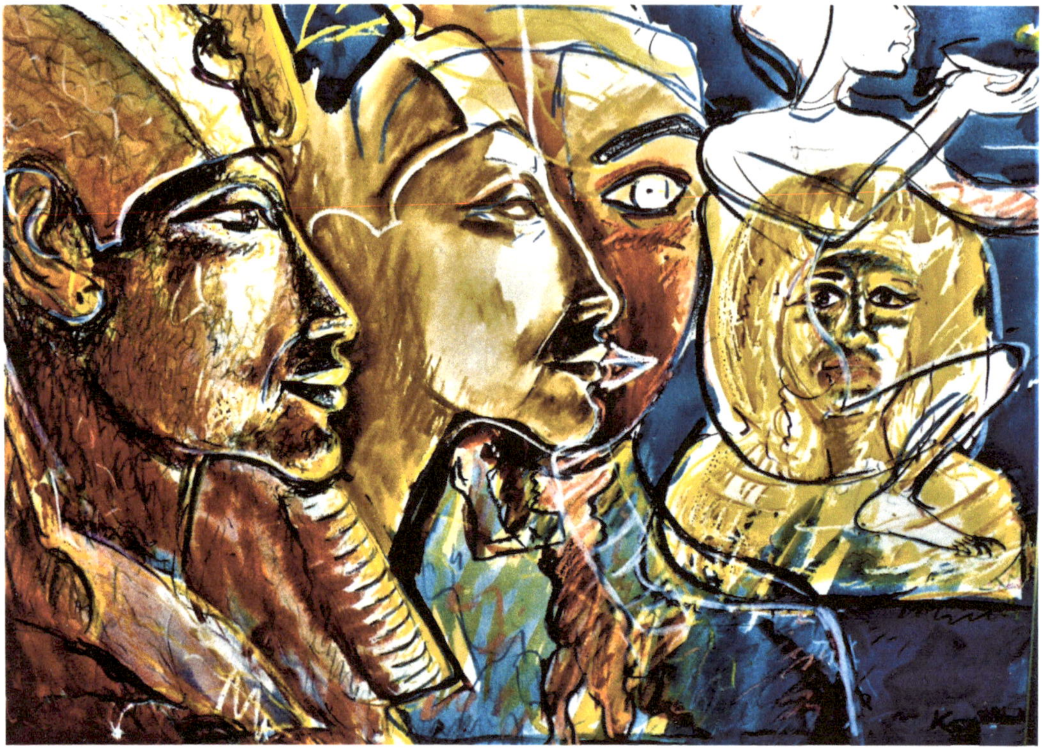

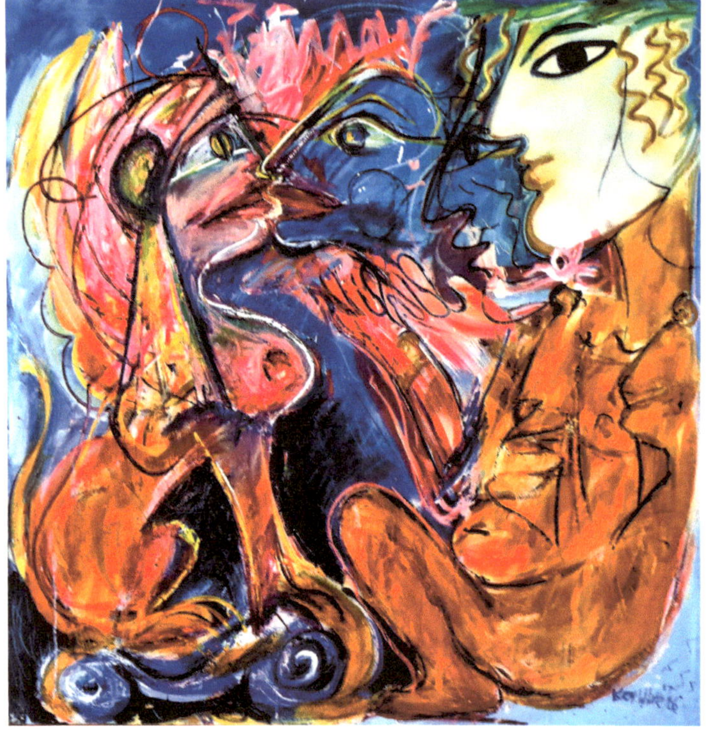

Above: *Akhnaten.*

Left: *Egypt.*

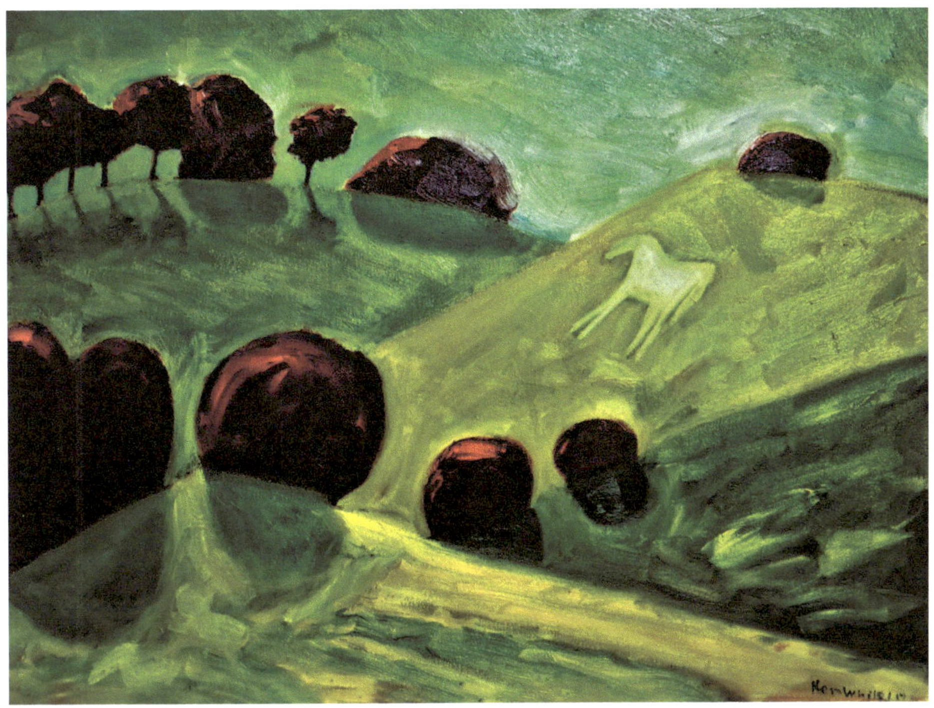

White Horse.

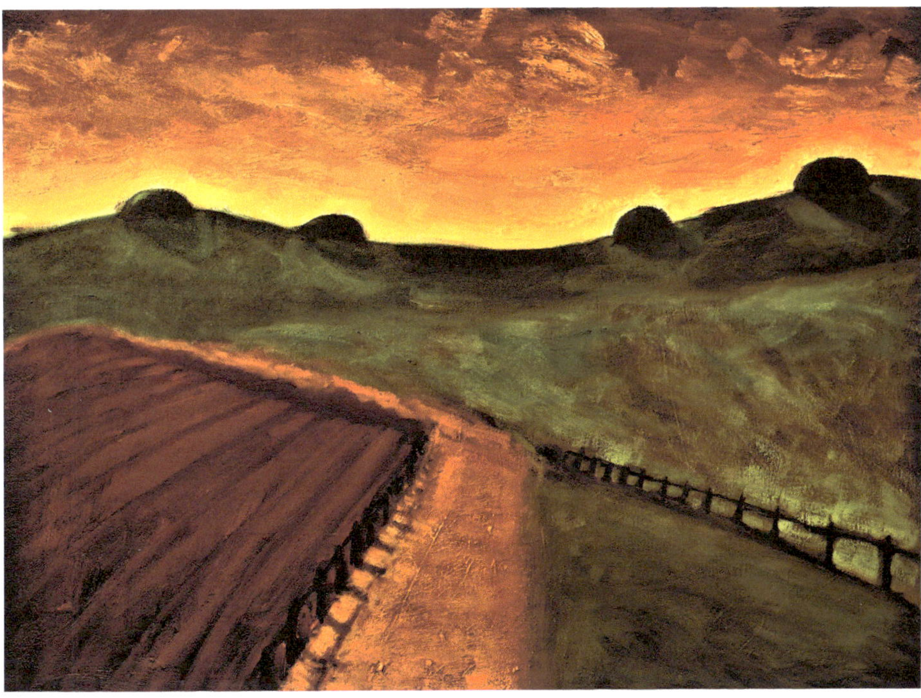

Wiltshire Landscape.

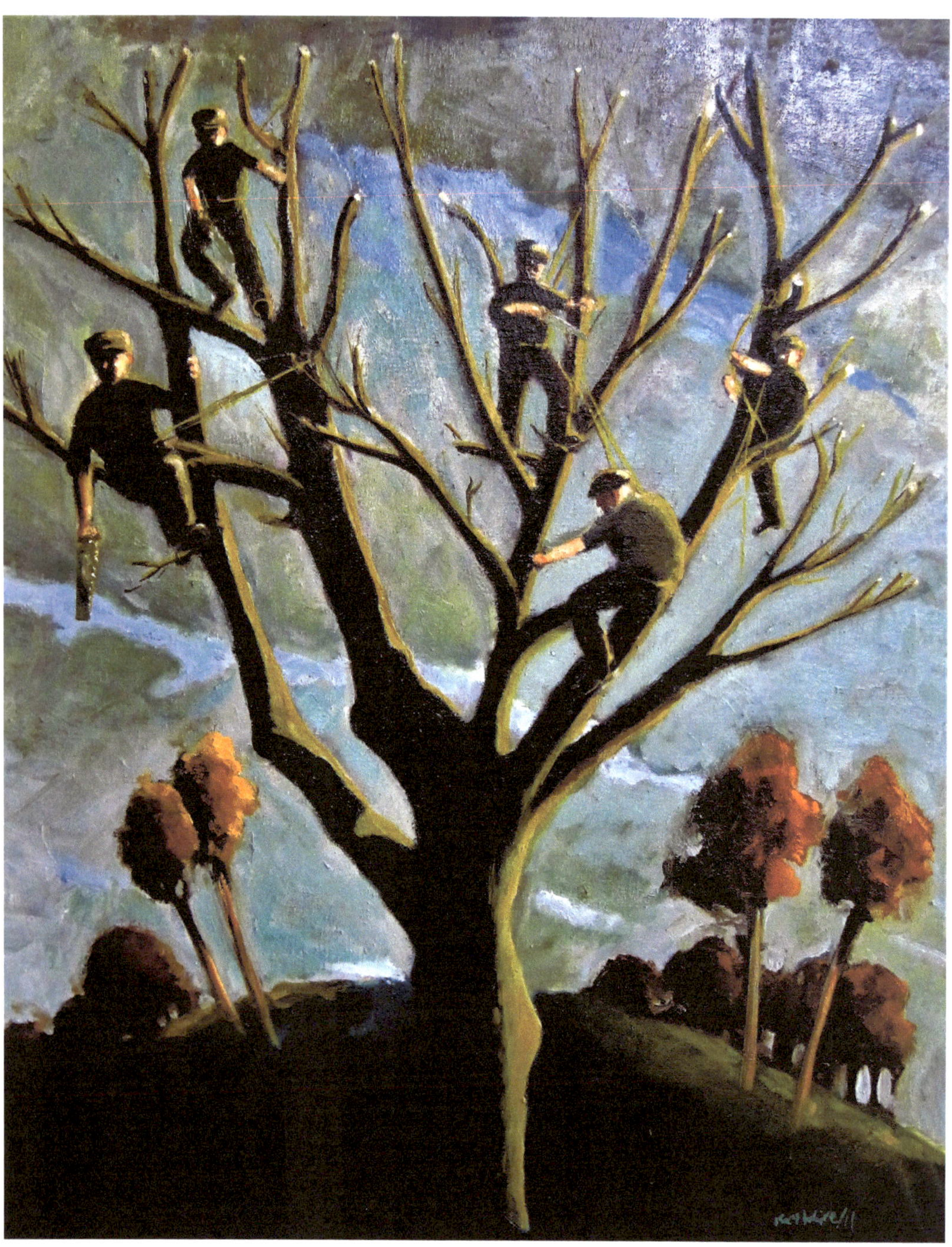

Tree Cutters.

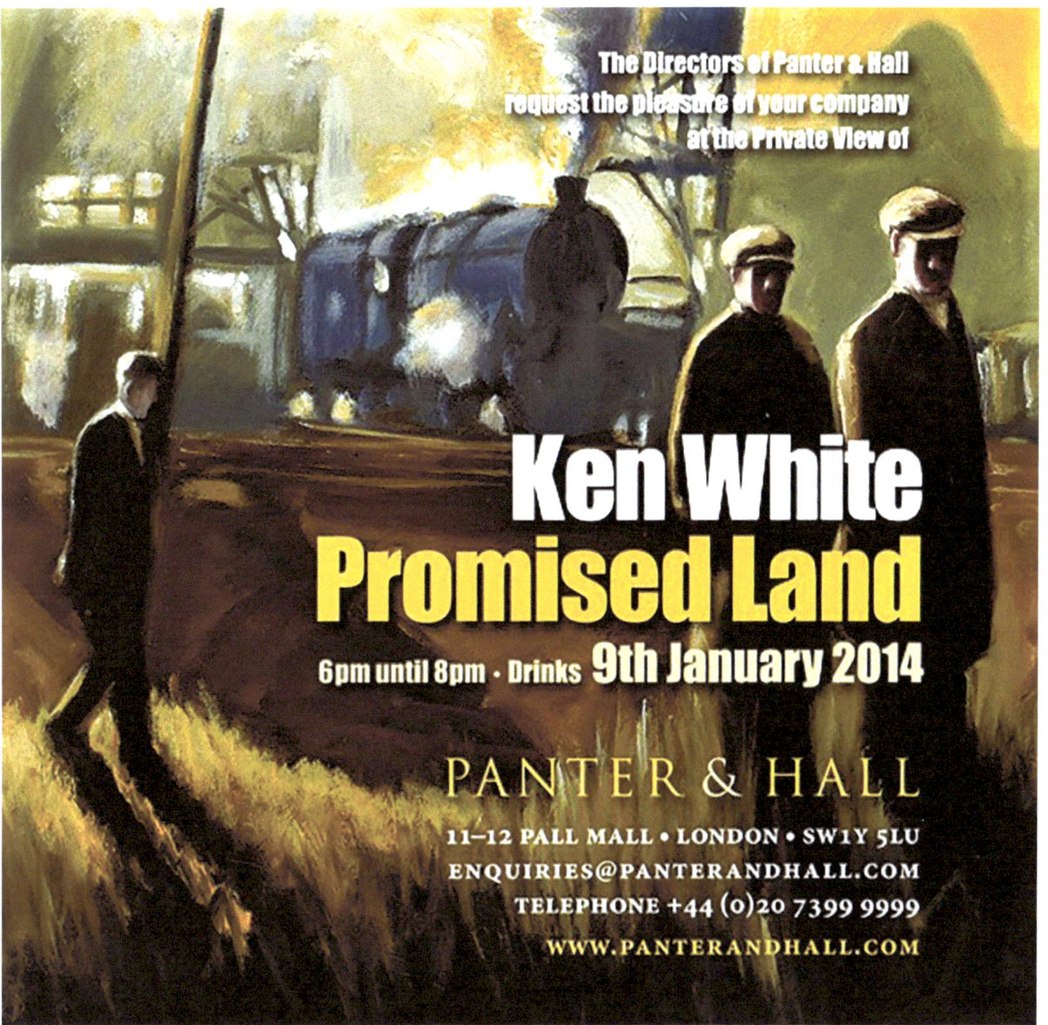

'Ken White – Promised Land', a Panter & Hall exhibition.

Appendix: A List of Ken's Murals

The date is the year of completion.

For Arts Organisations:

1. Golden Lion Bridge, Swindon, Wiltshire: 1976 – 25x25
2. Steam Train, Swindon, Wiltshire: 1976 – 30x100
3. Swindon Personalities (Famous Faces), Swindon, Wiltshire: 1979 – 25x25
4. Smith and Wellstood Building, Bonnybridge, Scotland: 1980 – 30x100
5. Cambria Bridge, Swindon, Wiltshire: 1982 – 27x200
6. Volunteer's Mural – Tom Fessey, Swindon, Wiltshire: 1982 – 25x25
7. Southampton Hospital Arts Project, waiting room: 1987
8. Southampton Hospital Corridor: 1989 – 200
9. Oxford Art Week: Akhenaten: 1990 – 8x12
10. Orthopaedic Room, Southampton Hospital: 1990

For Off the Wall:

Invergordon, Scotland: 2004 – 14x40
Invergordon, Scotland: 2005 – 26x26
Saltburn Mural, Invergordon, Scotland: 2007 – Gable end and two panels

For Local Authorities:

1. Castle Mural, Basing Street, Kensington, London
2. Oasis Leisure Dome, Swindon, Wiltshire
3. Brunel Shopping Centre, Swindon, Wiltshire
4. Cavendish Square, Swindon, Wiltshire
5. Highworth Swimming Pool, Highworth, Wiltshire

6. Kensington and Chelsea Swimming Pool, London
7. Trompe-l'œil Mural, Plymouth, Devon
8. Exhibition Building, Sussex, Canada

For Hospitals:

Princess Margaret Hospital, Swindon, Wiltshire
Great Western Hospital, Swindon, Wiltshire

For *She Magazine*:

Paint Your Own Mural

For Sound and Media:

XS Record Store, Street, Somerset
XS Record Store, Cheshire Oaks
Chester XS Record Store, Fleetwood, Lancashire
XS Record Store, Surrey
XS Record Store, Loch Laman, Scotland

For Virgin:

The Town House, Goldhawk Road, London
Venue Club, Victoria, London
Sex Pistols *The Great Rock 'n Roll Swindle*, Shepherd's Bush, London
Mike Oldfield *Incantations*, Shepherd's Bush
London Virgin Mansions, Ladbroke Grove, London
Victoria Pub, Uxbridge Road, London
Goldiggers Club, Chippenham, Wiltshire
Scarlet Lady, Virgin Atlantic Aeroplaces
The Manor, Kidlington, Oxford
The Manor Mobile
Roof Garden, High Street, Kensington
Olympic Studios, Barnes, London
Maiden Japan 747 Jumbo Jet
Roof Gardens Restaurant, High Street, Kensington
London Roof Gardens,
West Palm Beach, Florida, USA
Gatwick Reception Rooms, Gatwick Airport
Virgin Megastore, Milan, Italy
Virgin Megastore, Frankfurt, Germany

Virgin Megastore, Vienna, Austria
Virgin Megastore, Berlin, Germany
Virgin Megastore, Amsterdam, Holland
Virgin Megastore, Los Angeles, USA
Heathrow Upper Class Lounge, Heathrow Airport
Middlesex Virgin Megastore, Hamburg, Germany
Virgin Megastore, Los Angeles, USA
Virgin Megastore, Costa Masa, Orange County
USA Roof Gardens, High Street, Kensington, London
Mickleover Hotel, Derbyshire
Cwrt Bleddyn Hotel, Wales
Virgin Atlantic Lounge, JFK Airport, New York, USA
La Residencia Hotel, Mallorca
Virgin Megastore, Bergamo, Italy
Virgin Atlantic Offices, Norwalk, Connecticut, USA Virgin Megastore, Brussels, Belgium
Virgin Megastore, Vigo, Spain
Virgin Megastore, La Caroña, Spain
Virgin Megastore, Madrid, Spain
Virgin Megastore, Malaga, Spain
Virgin Lounge, Newark Airport, New Jersey, USA
Virgin Lounge, Heathrow Airport, Middlesex
Mickleover Hotel, Derbyshire
V2 Studios, London
Virgin Atlantic Offices, Norwalk, Connecticut, USA
XS Record Store, Swindon, Wiltshire
Virgin Megastore, Maastricht, Holland
Buxted Park Hotel, East Sussex
Virgin Atlantic Office, Norwalk, Connecticut, USA
Le Petit Blanc Restaurant, Cheltenham, Gloucestershire
Le Petit Blanc Restaurant, Manchester

Privately Sponsored or Business-Sponsored Murals:

Lethbridge School Mural
Swindon Fish Restaurant
Marlborough Indian Restaurant
Swindon Utopia Studios, London
Garden Wall Mural, Kensington Mews
London Guildford Market Murals, Guildford, Surrey
Gilberts Hill School, Swindon
Mercat Murals, Kirkcaldy, Scotland
History of Bodybuilding, Forest Gate, London
Sutton Manor, Sutton Scotney, Hampshire
Chinese Screens, Woking
Ken Kitchen Mural, Highworth

Wiltshire Bodybuilders Gym, Swindon, Wiltshire
Helston Aeropark, Cornwall
Vulture's Perch, Kentish Town
London Intercontinental Hotel, Park Lane, London
Madam Tussauds, London
Swimming Pool Mural, Guildford, Surrey
Great Western Hospital, Swindon, Wiltshire
St Margaret's School, Calne, Wiltshire
Great Western Hospital, Swindon, Wiltshire
The Gun Public House, Cold Harbour, London
Wyvern Theatre, Swindon, Wiltshire
Austin Leisure, Swindon, Wiltshire
Lydiard Park, Lydiard Tregoze, Swindon, Wiltshire

Books Illustrating Work by Ken White:

Aldridge, Alan, *Beatles Illustrated Lyrics* (Macdonald)
Ball, Richard and Andy Pittaway, *The Whole House Omnibus* (Astragal Books)
Barthelmeh, Volker, *Street Murals* (Penguin)
British Council Social Communication
Cooper, Graham and Doug Sargent, *Painting the Town* (Phaidon)
Crosby, Theo, *Art & Architecture Second Register of Artists and Craftsmen* (A&A)
Damase, Jacques (ed.), *L'Art Public* (Damase)
Design Council, *Streets Ahead* (Whitney Library of Design)
Evening Advertiser, *Images of Swindon* (Breedon)
Fassaden-Fantasien, Farbige, *Wand Art* (Klinkhardt & Biermann)
Giusti, Annamaria, *Arte E Illusione* (Giunti)
Hayes, Colin, *The Complete Gude to Painting & Drawing Techniques & Materials* (Phaidon)
Hillman, Judy, *The Rebirth of Covent Garden* (GLC)
Losifidis, Kiriakos, *Mural Art Vol. 2* (Publikat)
Lucie-Smith, Edward, *Art in the Seventies* (Phaidon)
Miles, Malcolm, *Art for Public Places* (Winchester School of Art Press)
Perec, George and Cuchi White, *L'Oeil Bloui* (Chene/Hachette)
Petherbridge, Deanna, *Art for Architecture* (HMSO)
Townsend, Peter, *Art Within Reach* (Thames & Hudson)
Webb, Linda and Jeffrey, *Beatles Art* (Boxigami Books)